Life
ALONG THE
Hudson

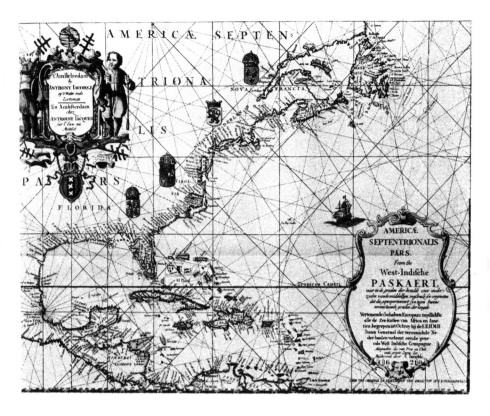

NEW NETHERLAND, 1621

This map, entitled "Americæ Septentrionalis Pars," was made by
A. Jacobsen for the Dutch West India Company in 1621. It
shows New Netherland and the Atlantic coastline of North and
Central America. Only a very small portion of the Hudson River
beyond its mouth appears on this map.

NEW NETHERLAND IN THE TIME OF MINUIT

From a survey made sometime during the period 1626-1632, while Peter Minuit was Director, the map opposite, of New Netherland was produced c. 1665 by Johannes Vingboon (variant spellings of his name appear as Vingboons and Vingboom). This map shows a much greater portion of the Hudson River, here labeled "De Noorde Rivier" or North River. A modern map showing the full length of the Hudson River serves as the Frontispiece in this volume.

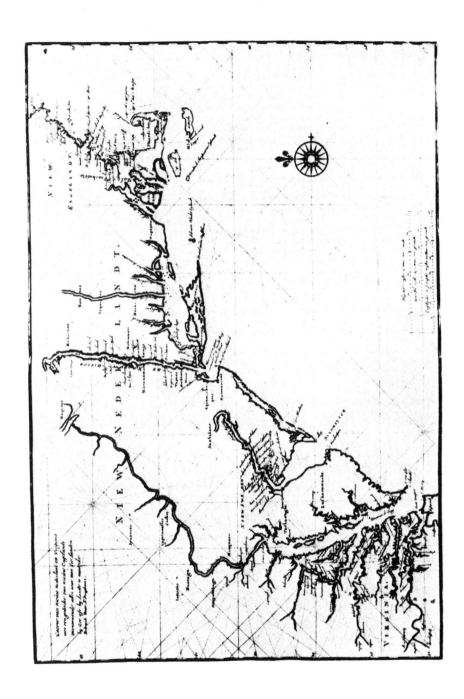

LIFE
ALONG THE
HUDSON

by

ALLAN KELLER

FORDHAM UNIVERSITY PRESS
New York
1997

Illustrations courtesy of Historic Hudson Valley,
successor of Sleepy Hollow Restorations, Inc.

Library of Congress Cataloging-in-Publication Data

Keller, Allan.
    Life along the Hudson / by Allan Keller.
        p.   cm.
    Originally published: Tarrytown, N.Y. : Sleepy Hollow
Restorations, © 1976.
    Includes bibliographical references (p.   ) and index.
    ISBN 0-8232-1803-1 (hc : alk. paper). — ISBN 0-8232-1804-X (pbk.
: alk. paper)
    1. Hudson River Valley (N.Y. and N.J.)—History.   2. River boats—
Hudson River.   I. Title.
F127.H8K38   1997
974.7'3—dc21   97-25054
                                                                   CIP

Printed in the United States of America

Table of Contents

List of Illustrations

List of Illustrations

List of Illustrations

List of Illustrations

Foreword

Allan Keller stated emphatically: "This volume is not a history. It is a set of kaleidoscopic impressions of life along the Hudson." And marvelous impressions they are, with all the colorful variation of a kaleidoscope. Yet through them, willy-nilly, this veteran journalist created a history line that would not be denied—like manifest destiny, like the new railroad of the 1840s, cutting through the front yards of the palatial homes along the river, upsetting plans for a quiet life on the water.

Keller died in 1981, after thirty-four years as reporter, feature writer, columnist, and editor for the *New York World Telegram*, followed by fourteen more years writing books and teaching at the Columbia University School of Journalism. This book was originally published in 1976, the year of the nation's bicentennial celebration. Fordham University Press was wise in choosing to republish it, one of our finest treatments of Hudson River life and history in all its complexity.

With a rich text and 98 carefully chosen and carefully interposed illustrations, the book advances chronologically from the early 1600s well into the twentieth century, and geographically north from New Amsterdam to Lake Tear of the Clouds, with exciting doublings back and revisits along the route. Then, after ten

Foreword

chapters of narration and description, it glides into a travelogue entitled "These Stately Mansions," providing the reader of today a list of places to visit to experience vicariously much of the human life of the centuries described earlier. This is followed by a short chapter on the search for the source of the Hudson, and then an "Epilogue" on threats to the river's environment.

Those ten chapters that are the heart of the book are just what we might expect from a craftsman like Keller: stand-alone feature articles on the period at hand, each with what professionals would call its own "slant." Thus, the first chapter, "The Adventure of Henry Hudson," while it gives us some of the basic facts on the explorer's activities, deals more with the beauty of the world he sailed, the sweetness of its air, and the productivity of the waters. It also gives details of the "Algonkian" people whose lives Hudson's visit permanently disrupted.

The second chapter, entitled "In the Days of the Dutch," emphasizes the difficulties of establishing European settlements and commerce in and around the area we now call Manhattan. Keller's presentations of the differing management styles of Governors Minuit, Kieft, and Stuyvesant have a familiar ring to those of us who have lived through the administrations of Mayors La-Guardia, Koch, and Giuliani and Governors Cuomo and Pataki. With the help of Washington Irving, Keller conducts us into the lives of the people living under the Dutch governors with their exalted titles. We see their churches, their homes, their superstitions, their trades, and their businesses and the solid beginnings of the New York we know today.

"The English Take Over," which follows, is an adroit narration of a momentous series of events, accomplished with little bloodshed. In the hands of the British the colony prospered, as it might have under the Dutch but didn't. Seventeenth-century manorial capitalism had come to the rescue, in the saddles and coaches of men named Philipse, Van Cortlandt, Schuyler, Livingston, and Van Rensselaer. These men and their descendants would shape the Hudson Valley that became part of the new nation over a century later, assisted by a mix of "Germans, Huguenots, Walloons, Englishmen and a dozen other nationalities [as they] swapped recipes, helped each other at barn railings, played together and often prayed together out of necessity." The description of Frederick Philipse's office and grist mill "near the mouth of the Pocantico River" reminds us of the more recent dominance of the Rockefeller family in that area, and informs us again that the influence of great families—like Rockefeller and Roosevelt and Vanderbilt and perhaps Fish and Kennedy—continues in the region.

In "The War of Independence" the Hudson Valley becomes the dominant theater of war, with particular emphasis on field events at Ticonderoga, West Point, and New York City. This chapter is a miraculously compressed account of the conflict, in thirty pages of pictures and words. Aspiring students of the American Revolution are advised to begin here.

Keller devotes two chapters to water travel in "From Sloop to Steamer" and "The Time of the Barges." The first shows well what it was like to travel on the sloops and packets and freight boats, and later on Robert Fulton's creations, as sail travel shifted to steam travel. The second shows the opulence of the barges which carried passengers a safe distance from the unstable steam engine and the confusions of the main vessel and afforded them opportunity to sleep or to dine, notably on shad, or to watch the busy river scene of passing boats and fishermen at work, or the panorama of mountain and village onshore.

The seventh chapter shows well the newspaperman Keller at work, as he skillfully compresses the masses of lore that could ordinarily come under the title "The Erie Canal" into a narration of the details of one event: the movable celebration of the opening of the canal as the towboat *Seneca Chief* set out from Buffalo on October 26, 1825, loaded with dignitaries, two kegs of Lake Erie water, and assorted symbols of the opening West, on a triumphal voyage by way of countless stops en route that would not be denied, accompanied by vessels great and small, to Sandy Hook for a "marriage of the waters." This essay gives the author an opportunity to discourse on the various products manufactured along the river course and to slide smoothly into the great industry of ice production.

Foreword

The title of the eighth chapter, "The Iron Horse," is almost trite, but the context is far from that, as Keller takes his reader from the Poughkeepsie docks in the winter of 1831, with boats loaded with perishable beef and pork "frozen in solid" by a sudden cold northwest wind and freezing temperatures, and the call of Matthew Vassar, founder of the college, for a Hudson Valley railroad. The riverbank was the obvious route for the trainbed; after all, that is where the towns were. But it was also where the great homes were, to say nothing of the mountainous shore. Terrain and local protest were surmounted, however, and the new era in river transportation began, to the delectation of some and the dismay of others.

The ninth chapter, "Of Palaces and Pleasures," is concerned mostly with the Catskill Mountain House and the Saratoga spa but at the end moves adroitly into a history of the river regatta, which originated in Saratoga and saw its greatest days in Poughkeepsie. Then, the tenth chapter collects many of the interesting minds and personalities of the region into one exciting discussion named "Dreamers, Doers, Shakers, and Others." Authors, reformers, architects, poets, painters: all come together in this chapter to build or buy or gaze afar at those "Stately Mansions" of the eleventh chapter, which have been referred to earlier.

An "Epilogue" ends the book on a hopeful note after discussion of environmental hazards to the river, but its reference to "the pernicious poisoning of unseen chemicals" shows that Keller was aware even in 1976 that some terrible environmental catastrophe could be just around the corner. And indeed it was, for his edition was published only shortly before the discovery of the hazard that still dominates assessments of water quality: the polychlorinated biphenyls, or PCBs, which have been traced primarily to the General Electric plants at Fort Edward and Hudson Falls. The contamination is particularly heavy from Hudson Falls as far as the dams at Troy, but can be found in disturbing strength from that point south throughout the river. The debate over what should be done with the PCBs—whether to dredge them or leave them alone and who should pay and how much—goes on and will go on undoubtedly for years more as superfunds lie barely tapped and warnings to fishermen and fish-consumers continue.

Keller was aware of the problem at Cold Spring's Foundry Cove, site of an old iron foundry where a battery plant more recently left residues of highly toxic cadmium. Doing something about this site has at least moved into the planning stage. He was not aware of the introduction of the zebra mussel and its capacity to foul water intake ducts. Various newer reports of encouraging sightings and counts of other river species, like the sturgeon and the shad, come out periodically; but, in general, Keller's "Epilogue" is as fresh a statement as one will find in the turbulent archives of Hudson River sanitation.

Outwardly, the river scene looks better and better. The shores which were logged off a century ago are rich in vegetation. The roofs and spires of many of the great homes are visible to viewers on either shore. The railroad journey is rewarding for one who has the wit to sit on the shore side. Some of the beaches are open again for swimming by the less squeamish. Marinas dot both banks. Shad are available at restaurants—some of them right by the shore. Boat trips, some overnight and longer, are available. Study trips and elderhostels abound. Allan Keller's Hudson is there for the taking, and in these pages the delight for the visitor, studious or simply curious, is immeasurably deepened.

Alfred H. Marks
1997

Life
ALONG THE
Hudson

Preface

A river is one of the truly exciting natural phenomena. From some minuscule beginning, a rift in the rocks, an Alpine meadow that catches rain from passing showers, or a bubbling spring, is born, first, a tiny rill, then a noisy brook, and finally a full-fledged river. When ultimately it empties into the sea, we see a whole new phase of its cycle. Its waters, drawn into the atmosphere by solar attraction, are then once again scattered across the face of the earth, some of that moisture returning as rain back at the site of its own beginnings.

The Hudson River is born in a pocket on the side of Mount Marcy, a thousand feet below the summit of the highest peak in the Adirondack mountain chain, a water-filled dimple that the Indians lyrically named: Lake Tear of the Clouds. It swiftly winds its way downhill through birch and hemlock, ash and maple, cutting through rocky chasms and chattering over pebbly beds until it reaches the verdant lowlands. Then it meanders between lush meadows and undulating pastures until, below West Point, it meets the Highlands.

In some ancient upheaval millions of years ago, it broke through this mountain barrier to run, alternately checked or aided by the ebb and flow of tidal wash, between steep escarp-

3

ments and basaltic palisades to where it meets the sea, in from Ambrose Light. Here, the dividing line between river and ocean is indistinct. Over the ages, the Hudson has cut a canyon on the floor of the continental shelf deep beneath the surface of the sea, as if to say, "even hundreds of miles from shore I am still a river."

Estimated to be seventy-five million years old, the Hudson is one of the great waterways of the world. Dixon Ryan Fox called it "that spacious and magnificent fjord"; to Carl Carmer it is "that free and mighty river." Along its banks human beings for centuries have enjoyed the blessings of riverine plenty and beauty. The native Indians at times ignored its charm, when it became a strategic military route in conflicts between inland and seashore tribes; but they never forgot that it was a basic source of their livelihood. The white man, once he had accepted the fact that it would not lead to the Orient and great wealth, learned to love it for itself, established cities and built fine homes upon its shores; and in the course of time it provided riches that would have dazzled Henry Hudson, its first white discoverer. The river served again as a vital military highway during the American Revolutionary War; then in the era of commercial and industrial expansion as a major component of the Hudson-Erie Canal-Great Lakes corridor to the Middle and Far West. Where it meets the sea it has seen the New World's largest metropolis arise, reach toward the sky, and spread across the land.

This volume is not a history. It is a set of kaleidoscopic impressions of life along the Hudson, from earliest days to the present. It does not purport to be exhaustive or complete. Rather it is a collection of images caught in the mirror of time, as seen by one who, raised beside the Shetucket River, has come to love the Hudson.

Prefaces are convenient for authors who wish to explain their thinking about what they have written. They are equally useful as a means of acknowledging the assistance of others in the book's preparation. My considerable debt is owed to many, but particularly these: Mrs. Henry T. Birgel and Mrs. Elisha Keeler of the Darien Library; Mrs. William Therrien and Mrs.

Preface

Mary Lawson of Sleepy Hollow Restorations; Robert H. Boyle of the Hudson River Fishermen's Association; and, most of all, my wife, who was with me all the way.

ALLAN KELLER
1976
Darien, Connecticut

HENRY HUDSON'S SHIP, THE *Half Moon*

Henry Hudson's first mate, Robert Juet, kept a log in which he recorded that Indians came aboard the *Half Moon* as it sailed up what was later to be known as the Hudson River. This engraving of the *Half Moon* is from Hollyer's *Old New York Views*.

Chapter I

The Adventure of Henry Hudson

To the men on Henry Hudson's *Half Moon*, the Indian birch-bark canoes must have seemed like elfin craft. Bobbing in the waves at the mouth of the river, where the tide stood in from the sea, they were as cockleshells beside the stout-timbered, unwieldy Dutch vessel. On that morning of September 4, 1609, there was no one else to mark the symbolism of this encounter. Yet, within a century, it was to spell destruction to the native civilization.

It took the river Indians, perhaps Manhattas or Wappingers, eight or ten days to fashion their frail craft, skillfully shaping vines and adding pitch to hold the strips of bark together. In the Dutch shipyard across the Atlantic, scores of men using iron tools, hand-forged nails, and metal stripping, had laboriously fashioned the *Half Moon* over a period of months. The beauty of the frail canoes could never match the practicality of the heavy-timbered ship. When the onward surge of the Europeans was set in motion after Henry Hudson left "the mayne ocean" and entered the river, neither the Dutch nor the Indians could have realized that what was to be known as the Hudson River would never be the same again.

Giovanni da Verrazano, the Florentine explorer in the service of the King of France, had sailed past the mouth of the river in 1524, almost a century before. Poking into one inlet after another along the American littoral, he actually entered Lower

New York Bay but he did not attempt to investigate further. On his return to Europe, he described the "River of Steep Hills" to the French king and told how he had sent a small boat into the narrows, been hailed by natives who looked like most of the others he had seen farther south, and then quit the area hurriedly when contrary winds began to blow. He wrote that he had discovered "a very agreeable site located within two small prominent hills [the Narrows], in the midst of which flowed to the sea a very big river, which was deep within the mouth." Others, probably including Portuguese, English, and Dutch, may have seen the River of Steep Hills, but they left little trace of their visits.

So it was Henry Hudson, the English captain sailing for the Dutch West India Company, who first undertook the serious exploration of this river. We can speculate that sweet scents and perfumes, blowing offshore from the mainland, helped persuade him that inland lay the route to the elusive Northwest Passage to Cathay. In a day when factory smokestacks, abattoirs, chemical factories, refineries, and sewage plants pollute the air and send nauseating stenches across the land, it is hard to imagine how attractive the country must have been three centuries ago. Sailors who had been too long at sea marveled at the New World's scented air. Columbus noticed it, John Winthrop likened the New England air to "the smell of a garden," and Sir Walter Raleigh's colonists detected the odors of wild flowers and blooming shrubs before the Outer Banks rose up on the western horizon.

What was later to be called New York Bay, must have recalled a Veronese landscape to Hudson and his men. As they sailed into the Upper Bay, a jewel box of a landlocked harbor, the high hills of Staten Island, the heavily forested shores of Manhattan, Brooklyn, Governor's Island, and the New Jersey coastline were a welcome contrast to their earlier landfalls. For several years, Hudson, in the employ of English companies, had tried to find a way to the Spice Islands by sailing above Europe, skirting the barren foreshores of Norway, Novaya Zemlya, and Spitzbergen. Now, on this journey under Dutch auspices, he had sailed first

HENRY HUDSON

This seventeenth century British school portrait said to be of Henry Hudson is in the collections of Sleepy Hollow Restorations.

along Nova Scotia and Cape Cod, before he reached this river. Oaks, chestnuts, and hickory trees grew in profusion; and where the land was low, green meadows stretched away like beckoning fingers between the hills. Seals splashed on the rocks at Robbins Reef where the ferry now passes and sturgeon and salmon were so plentiful they could be caught without bait.

Hudson was so eager to believe that at last he had found a body of water which could carry him to Cathay that he continued his quest above Manhattan Island. Indians came to barter with his men, but before he was out of sight of the Narrows, there was friction with some of the local tribes; men were killed on both sides. It was hardly an auspicious beginning for his trip upriver. The *Half Moon* proceeded north on September 12, passed where Yonkers is today, after the sailors purchased a mess of plump oysters from more friendly Indians, threaded the reaches of the Highlands, and by September 18 had reached a point where even Hudson realized the river was not a Northwest Passage to the Orient.

The navigator sent small boats ashore several times but it would appear that he himself did not land until that afternoon, when the *Half Moon* was in the shallows above present-day Castleton. Back on board, he wrote of his visit to an Indian village, but there was no hint of disappointment about the shattered dream. Instead, he recorded that the place was

> . . . the finest for cultivation that I ever in my life set foot upon, and it also abounds in trees of every description. . . . It is as pleasant a land as one can tread upon, very abundant in all kinds of timber suitable for ship-building, and for making large casks. The people had copper tobacco pipes, from which I inferred that copper must exist there; and iron likewise according to the testimony of the natives, who, however, do not understand preparing it for use.

The next day, Hudson pushed on to where Albany now stands, dropped anchor, and sent the ship's boat upriver. It must have been a tragic hour for him. He had noted the shallowing of the

Museum of the City of New York

MANHATTA INDIAN VILLAGE

The scene in a village of the Manhatta Indian tribe before the time of Dutch exploration might have appeared as in this diorama created by Ned Burnes for the Museum of the City of New York.

channel, sensed the weakening of the tidal flow, and knew by the simple test of taste that the river had lost virtually all of its salinity. When the small boat returned with word that neither the parent stream nor its tributary, the Mohawk, was navigable, the captain knew that once again his hopes for a route to China had been dashed.

Henry Hudson's log was lost, except for a few scattered excerpts included in a later account of the voyage written by the Belgian-born geographer, Johannes de Laet. What we know of his voyage up the Hudson in 1609 comes mainly from a log kept by one of his mates, Robert Juet of "Lime-house." There was no doubt in Juet's mind that they had fallen upon a beautiful country. At the close of the very first entry made by Juet, while the *Half Moon* was lying at anchor off Staten Island, the sailor wrote: ". . . this is a very good land to fall with, and a pleasant land to see." He reports pleasant weather, good winds to propel the ship, and enchanting scenes on either side of the river. The Indians behaved with little consistency, some acting generously and well, and others trying to steal goods from the deck or firing arrows at the crew. The behavior of the upriver natives was better than that of those nearer the sea. Hudson went ashore to dine with one group and described the meeting as follows: "The natives are a very good people; for when they saw that I would not remain, they supposed that I was afraid of their bows, and taking the arrows, they broke them in pieces, and threw them into the fire. . . . " Several Indian maidens came aboard the *Half Moon* and Juet reported that they "behaved themselves very modestly." On another occasion, Indian men brought a huge bark tray full of roasted venison to the ship, watched the Europeans eat, and then paid reverence to Hudson as a person of almost godlike stature.

These aborigines along the river were Algonkians, a loose confederacy of Indians reaching from the St. Lawrence River down to Virginia. Those who dwelt hard by the Hudson belonged to many sub-tribes; the Mahicans situated on the northern reaches, the Delawares west of the river below the Catskills, and the Wappingers settled along the river from about modern

Poughkeepsie down to the sea and along part of Long Island Sound. The Mahicans, like other woodland Indians in general, were less warlike than their neighbors to the north and west, the Iroquois, and lived a comfortable life hunting in the deep woods, fishing in the Hudson, and raising vegetables such as corn, pumpkins, squash, and beans. There was venison aplenty; squirrels and rabbits were everywhere, wild turkey strutted in the woodland glens, and flocks of passenger pigeons supplied food for every campfire. Millions of beavers provided warm clothing for winter, and the skins of the deer served for everyday wear.

A searching hiker, following the river shore today, might come upon kitchen middens where generations of Indians threw their empty oyster shells. Some of these middens are twelve feet deep—not surprising, since there were once vast oyster beds in the Hudson from the lower bay to Croton Point. Heath hen, now virtually extinct (except for a few that may survive on the sandy wastes of Martha's Vineyard), were as abundant as chickens. Geese, mallard, canvasbacks, and teal on stream and pond were easily caught, and the waters of the river itself were alive with striped bass, perch, and that great delicacy, shad.

On the whole, life was relatively easy for the Indians in their scattered small villages along the tributaries and the big river. In the summer, they moved down to the shore of the main river to fish and raise their simple crops. In the winter, they moved inland to find sheltered valleys where rock outcroppings and dense forests shut out the cold northern wind. Although there was intertribal squabbling, the Algonkian tribes were not very warlike. By contrast, the Mohawks, far upcountry, were.

When the women were not busy cooking succotash or corn cakes, sewing clothes of deerskin, or baking clams in sand pits heated with hot stones and wrapped in seaweed, they helped the men build the wonderfully light and sturdy canoes of birchbark. They stripped a large section of the bark of a fullgrown birch, spread it on the ground, and lashed false gunwales on the material to give it shape. Then stakes were driven in to hold the sides in place, true gunwales lashed inside and outside with vines, and a lining of cedar strips laid in lengthwise. Finally, all joints were made watertight by the application of boiling spruce or fir pitch. Thwarts were lashed from side to side and fastened in their turn with vines so strong they could support two or three occupants at a time.

These Indians relied on turkey feathers, goose quills, and the tails of little animals for ornamentation. The exception was wampum: belts of colored beads laboriously cut from shells. The purple lining of the quahog clam was most highly prized, while ordinary beads were cut from white oyster and scallop shells. Here artistic expression and a desire to fashion a crude currency led the natives to labor long hours drilling holes in tiny chips of shell and braiding them into strands.

The Mahicans, Wappingers, Sint Sinks, Manhattas, and other river tribes had never seen anything like Henry Hudson's *Half Moon* on the Great River before. This craft moved without oars, driving before the wind that dappled the waters of the Tappan Zee, tacking through the narrow reaches of the Highlands as if by magic. Braves looking up from their work of shaping bows or patching moccasins must have marveled at the Dutch explorer's ship, and squaws hoeing the hills of corn with a clam fastened to a stick, or nursing their young beside the wigwam, watched in amazement.

Ever since the glaciers receded, this stream had been their own, knowing only the soft swish of paddle blade or the sharp slap of sturgeon and shad breaking the surface in quest of a darting insect. They watched the river foaming by in spring flood and flowing placidly in the late summer months. From their smoky but comfortable long houses they heard the grinding noise of ice floes when the first thaws came, and rejoiced that spring was on the way. All these manifestations of the river's patterns were familiar. Now there was something new. White men with strange clothing, with weapons that boomed and shot out fire and death, had invaded their river in a wind-driven craft hundreds of times larger than their canoes.

For some six thousand years, Algonkians had dwelt by the edge of the Hudson. Scientists know this from carbon 14 analysis of oyster shells dug from a kitchen midden on Croton Point.

During that passage of many centuries, little change had occurred among the Indians. One span of a hundred years differed hardly at all from the next. Generation followed generation, content to live by nature's bounty, barely stirring the fires of human progress. Not unlike the ceaseless flow of the river was their own existence. This stream that cut from the mountains to the sea they called *Muhheakunnuk* or "great waters constantly in motion". To them it was means of transportation, source of food, and, best of all, a place by which to lift their spirits.

Now, as the billowing sails of the *Half Moon* intruded on this scene of natural grandeur, change had finally come.

Chapter II

In the Days of the Dutch

News of the rich land waiting to be exploited along the river Hudson had discovered brought no sudden or lively response from the Dutch authorities in Amsterdam. Life in the Netherlands of the seventeenth century was pleasant. Dutch ships were busy all over the known world, Dutch merchants traded in all the continents, and Holland was enjoying what many historians describe as a golden age of culture and prosperity.

There had been a few half-hearted attempts to set up fur-trading posts, one of which was established on the present site of Albany; but it was not until 1623, when the little sailing vessel *New Netherlands* anchored off Manhattan Island, that the Dutch made a bid to establish a foothold on the American continent. Even then it was a timid, and nearly disastrous, venture. Thirty French-speaking Belgian Walloon families headed by the Dutch navigator, Cornelis May, gazing upon the finest harbor on the Atlantic coast, sensed that here might be a start for Dutch power in the New World. But they nearly spoiled the dream by spreading themselves too thin. Some families went ashore at Nutten Island Harbor (later Governor's Island), while others settled on Long Island, the Delaware River, or along the Connecticut River. A few joined the fur traders at their outpost at Fort Orange (renamed Albany by the British in 1664), 150 miles up the Hudson. Had the nearby Indians been Mohawks, such tiny enclaves might have been wiped out, however the

Algonkians allowed them to exist and eventually to grow larger.

Only eight men weathered the winter of 1623 on Nutten Island. Using a ship's boat left for the purpose, or borrowing birchbark canoes from their Manhatta Indian neighbors, they paid rare visits to other settlers living along the shores of what we now call Brooklyn and New Jersey.

Ships came and went occasionally to pick up beaver pelts and other furs along the Bay sites, and up the river, but fur traders were left mostly to their own devices until the next summer, when others arrived. Slowly, the little clusters of rough huts around the Upper Bay grew. Peter Minuit, the Rhenish Prussian who was named Director General of New Netherland, arrived in 1626 with a group of permanent settlers. At that time some two hundred Europeans were scattered in the area claimed by the Dutch (now New York, New Jersey, and parts of Delaware).

Minuit was the first appointed company leader on the scene. He is said to have traded sixty guilders' (twenty-four dollars in nineteenth century currency) worth of pretty cloth, hatchets, needles, fish hooks, and other trifles with the Indians for the island of Manhattan, and promptly named the settlement New Amsterdam. This historic barter scene was much more than a gala day in the life of the little colony. It marked an important step in the Dutch decision to pay the Indians for their land—a policy rewarded by fairly peaceful relations for some ten years.

The beaver etched on the official shield of New York City is more than symbolic. The business-minded burghers back home wanted profits from their venture into the New World and, except for gold and precious stones, nothing would prove more valuable at that time than furs. Settlements came into being to trade with the Indians for beaver pelts, and the forts established as outposts in Indian territory were primarily collection centers for the fur trade. In their economic priorities, the Dutch differed from the English in Virginia and Massachusetts Bay.

Following Hudson's expedition, various Dutch merchants had become active in the fur trade with the northern "Virginias,"

NEW AMSTERDAM, C. 1643

This copper engraving, *Nieu Amsterdam* (c. 1643), from a
seventeenth or eighteenth century collection, is said to be one of
the earliest known views of New York; the artist and engraver are
unknown. Visible in the background are some of the earliest
buildings constructed on Manhattan island, including those of
the Dutch West India Company.

as the territory was then designated. As early as 1614, the States-General of the Netherlands guaranteed to those discoverers "of new passages, havens, countries or places" a monopoly on the trade to that territory. Several independent merchants merged their efforts in that year to create the New Netherland Company. This was the first time this name was used to denote the region previously called "Virginias" (what would later become New York, New Jersey, Vermont, portions of Delaware and Connecticut, and the whole of Cape Cod).

In order to regulate the fur trade and bring order out of the dangerous rivalries between the Dutch merchants, the States-General in 1623 set up the Dutch West India Company, which was given the authority to rule. Faced with business losses from the onset, it soon offered to establish patroonships, or landed estates. These were offered to any Dutchman who would transport fifty able-bodied persons to New Netherland and set them to work tilling the soil, clearing the land, and supporting the fur trade. Such patroons could ask for and receive land in the Hudson Valley, or on the Connecticut or Delaware rivers. What is more, they possessed well-nigh feudal privileges, such as the right to appoint local officers and set up civil and criminal courts.

The Company had high hopes for this new arrangement, but to no avail. With one outstanding exception, Rensselaerswyck, all the patroonships failed. Reasons for failure were many: a shortage of skilled settlers, the cost of transportation and maintenance of the settlers, and the creation of private armies all militated against potential profits. Although the plan looked well-thought-out on paper, in practice it just did not work.

Part of the task confronting the West India Company was to establish a legitimate claim to the lands of New Netherland by right of possession. It was for this reason that the first hardy band was left on Nutten Island. But their cattle rapidly began to die off because of illness, and the group decided to abandon that place and settle elsewhere. Sometime between the Fall of 1625 and the Spring of 1626, the small group of settlers left Nutten and moved onto the larger island of Manhattan. The fact that they decided to make this their main settlement in the Bay reg-

20

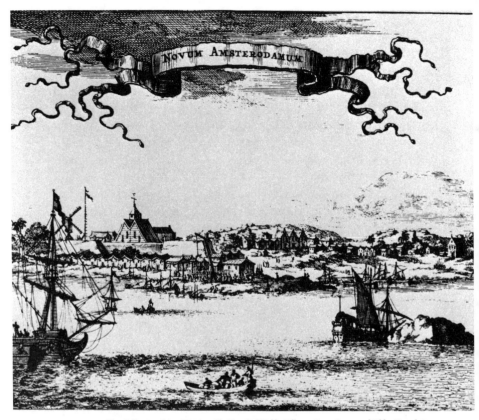

Eno Collection, Prints Division, The New York Public Library, Astor, Lenox and Tilden Foundations

NEW AMSTERDAM, c. 1650

The busy port of New Amsterdam, c. 1650, as rendered by the cartographer "Montanus." It was about this time that Frederick Philipse, later to become one of the wealthiest men in New York, arrived as a penniless carpenter from Holland.

21

ion accounted for Minuit's official purchase of the island from the Indians in 1626.

The town of New Amsterdam became a busy port almost immediately. Some idea of the type of cargoes in the harbor may be gleaned from the manifest of the *Arms of Amsterdam* which sailed for Holland with 7,246 beaver skins, 853 otter pelts, 853 skins of lynx, muskrat, and mink, and loads of walnut and oak timbers for the shipyards of the mother country. Many of the pelts came from communities in the salt marshes of Jersey, known by such names as Pavonia, a Latin form of the patroon's name, Paauw, or Communipaw, named for the same man but with a French linguistic twist, a deformation of the Gallic *Commune de Paauw*. Other furs came from far inland where the Dutch had outposts at Fort Orange, at the mouth of the Esopus on the Hudson, and in the Catskills.

Trade with the rising New England communities was also burgeoning. Much of the early success of the New Englanders was due to food and materials supplied to them by Dutch merchants via New Amsterdam. The Hudson itself was alive with maritime activity. Furs went downriver in small canoes, in larger war canoes transformed into freight carriers, in a few French-style bateaux, and in deep-sea ships that with little difficulty sailed far upriver.

Meanwhile New Amsterdam grew apace. Log huts were replaced with substantial wooden buildings which, in turn, gave way to stone and brick structures copied from older habitations in the Netherlands. With their crow-stepped gables and common walls, the houses looked as if they had been transported intact from Leyden, the Hague, and Rotterdam. Most of these buildings clustered around the stone fort near the present-day Battery, but closer to the East River were warehouses and barns holding furs, skins, trading goods, lumber, and flour.

Early cartographers differed in the maps supplied the new colony. The Indians had called the river that created the harbor Muhheakunnuk; Verrazano called it the River of Steep Hills. Officially the Dutch used the name Mauritius, after Prince Maurice, but usually they preferred the simpler one of North

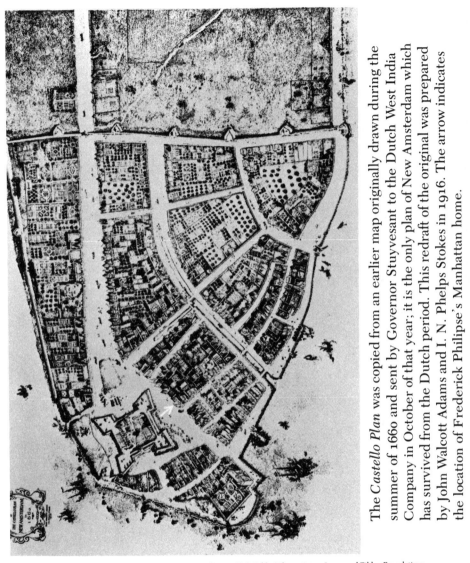

The *Castello Plan* was copied from an earlier map originally drawn during the summer of 1660 and sent by Governor Stuyvesant to the Dutch West India Company in October of that year; it is the only plan of New Amsterdam which has survived from the Dutch period. This redraft of the original was prepared by John Walcott Adams and I. N. Phelps Stokes in 1916. The arrow indicates the location of Frederick Philipse's Manhattan home.

I. N. Phelps Stokes Collection Prents Division The New York Public Library Astor, Lenox and Tilden Foundations

Castello Plan OF NEW AMSTERDAM, c. 1665–1670

River. Since they claimed all the land from the Delaware to the Connecticut, they called the former the South River and the latter the Fresh River. Only with the passage of time did the North River become Hudson's River, and then just the Hudson River; but even today in New York City the part adjacent to the island is known as the North River.

As more and more people came to the new land to seek fortune, the Dutch threw up few barriers to anyone seeking to become a colonist. Able-bodied men and women, along with their children, kept the ships moving, the pelts coming to the port, and the population increasing.

A notice published by the West India Company in Holland made it clear how anxious the authorities were for settlers:

> All good inhabitants of the Netherlands and all others inclined to plant colonies in New Netherland shall be at liberty to send three or four persons in the Company's ships going thither to examine the circumstances there, on condition that they swear to the articles, as well as the officers and seamen, as far as they relate to them, and pay for board and passage out and home, to wit, those who eat in the master's cabin, fifteen stivers per day, and those who go and eat in the orlop, shall have their board and passage gratis, and in case of an attack, offensive or defensive, they shall be obliged to lend a hand with the others, on condition of receiving, should any of the enemy's ships be overcome, their share of the booty pro rata, each according to his quality, to wit: the colonists eating out of the cabin shall be rated with the seamen, etc.,etc.

Enough early colonists were impressed by what they found in New Netherland to remain or to send for their families to join them. By the 1640's, the Hudson was a busy artery of Dutch commerce, teeming with small boats and ships, log rafts, and the ubiquitous birchbark canoes. New Amsterdam, a great lure for trade, was as a magnet drawing vessels from everywhere.

At first, except for an occasional brush or two, the Dutch

NEW YORK IN 1660

This illustration, c. 1855, entitled "New York in 1660," shows
Dutch colonists bartering with the Indians. The peg-legged man
in the center of the scene is presumably intended to represent
Peter Stuyvesant, the Dutch governor.

and Indians generally lived in peaceful coexistence around the rim of the harbor and up the Hudson. Trouble did come during the directorship of Governor Willem Kieft. A petty despot who ruled the colony with an iron hand for ten years (1638–1647), he was accused of stealing taxes for his personal use, licensing taverns throughout the town for his own profit, selling guns and powder to the Indians, and building a brewery across the river in Weehawken, in order to sell more liquor to the natives. Had these been his only transgressions, the people could have survived without much trouble. But, when he escalated a minor dispute with the Indians into an attack against one of their villages in Jersey, while ostensibly protecting them from the rival Mohawks, tribesmen took up arms along the river to seek revenge. Outlying Dutch homes were burned and their inhabitants killed. No small settlement was safe. Refugees crowded into the confines of Fort Amsterdam, fearing a general uprising that would sweep the colonists into the sea. Only timely intervention by militia from Connecticut and the subsequent arrival of a hundred men sent from Curaçao by Peter Stuyvesant prevented the annihilation of the Dutch colonists.

Peace returned to the Hudson Valley with Kieft's departure and in 1648 the colonists warmly welcomed Peter Stuyvesant as their new governor. Pelts started downriver again, new crops were put in at the outlying settlements, and shipbuilders went back to work on the Manhattan shores.

In such a busy port, building ships was now a necessity. With plenty of raw materials at hand, tall oaks for masts and main timbers, elm for decks, and other wood for sheathing, the colonists could build their own craft. By chance, we know about the first ship built in Manhattan, early in the period between Hudson's discovery and the arrival of the settlers under Cornelis May.

From shortly after the discovery, Dutch sea captains had carried on a lucrative trade with the Indians prior to establishment of the West India Company. Hendrick Christiansen had sailed up the Hudson and set up a small post called Fort Nassau on an island near present-day Albany. The Dutch explorer-merchant Adrian Block had been busy in Long Island Sound, discovering the island named after him and going up the Connecticut River as far as present-day Hartford. While Block was taking on food and fresh water at what is now Dey Street in lower Manhattan, his ship, the *Tiger*, caught fire and burned to the water's edge.

He put his crew to work building a replacement—a tiny sixteen-ton vessel barely adequate to take them back home across the Atlantic. He named her *Onrust*, or Restless. This was in the year 1613, and the little log cabin where he housed his men and the crude ways at the river's edge constituted the earliest shipyard in the area. Approximately forty-four feet long and eleven feet in beam, the *Onrust* was the first of a long line of ships to be built on the shores of the Hudson. Sandhogs digging a tunnel for the New York subway three centuries later, in 1916 uncovered the bottom portion of the burned ship's hull, exactly where historians said it had been destroyed. The fact that the find was made on Dey Street at Greenwich Street, two blocks from the river's edge, was not surprising: in Block's time, the shore had been at that point; it was filled in to the present bulkhead line much later.

In the Hudson Valley the river was virtually the only thoroughfare for half a century. People and goods moved predominantly by water. The first settlements hugged the river's edge, usually where a smaller stream entered, and roads were virtually unknown. Travel on foot was slow and arduous, and horseback travel hardly less so. The river was the safest, surest means of transportation. The fact that it was beautiful beyond belief, with wooded hills marching in serried ranks down to the water's edge, with the basaltic columns of the Palisades rising straight up from the shore and bucolic vistas stretching away on either side to the Catskills and the Taconic hills made its appeal even more compelling. Hollanders, used to the flat, dreary landscape of their homeland, with its monotonous polders and tight little fields, gazed with special awe and admiration at these sights, glorying in the virgin forests that clothed the hills beside the river. The scenery and charm of this lovely region undoubtedly made it easier for them to withstand the hard labor, the

shortages, the perils, and the wildness of their new home.
Wherever they settled, the Dutch pioneers found life arduous. In New Amsterdam, a few persons lived well, but most
dwelled in humble homes on streets which also served as open
sewers, where water had to be carried long distances, and where
the stench of decaying garbage along with the thousands of bales
of pelts turned summer days into misery.

But soon the new colony was to develop its own big entrepreneurs and wealthy men. In 1638, twelve years after the
purchase of Manhattan Island, a soldier in the service of the
West India Company, Oloff Stevense arrived from Holland. Ten
years later, he entered business for himself, added Van
Cortlandt to his patronymic, and within a surprisingly short time
was a rich man. Around 1653, a penniless carpenter, Frederick
Philipse—to use his Anglicized name—emigrated to the colony
as a workman in the employ of the West India Company. Before
he died, he owned a 90,000-acre manor in what is now
Westchester County, and a large section of the Bronx portion of
New York City. His lands extended from Spuyten Duyvil at the
northern end of Manhattan almost to the Croton River in
Westchester along the Hudson.

There were other landholdings along the Hudson, some
created out of the earlier patroonships, some purchased from the
Indians. These holdings had in common the need for able hands
to put in crops, fell trees for lumber, make barrels to hold flour,
or operate grist mills, and man the sloops that were the work-
horses of the Hudson River. As people moved upriver they
clung chiefly to the shores of the main stream or clustered in villages where tributaries flowed into the larger one. At first, they
were understandably loath to go far inland except on hunting
trips.

Johannes de Laet, writing in 1625, had thought the Hudson
Valley was an ideal place for Dutch settlement. He wrote home:

The country is well adapted for our people to inhabit, on
account of the similarity of the climate and the weather to
our own; especially since it seems to lack nothing that is

LANDS OWNED BY FREDERICK PHILIPSE

Between the time of his arrival in New Amsterdam around 1653 and his death in 1702, Frederick Philipse acquired some 90,000 acres of land in what is today Westchester County and part of the Bronx. The shaded portion of this contemporary map of the region shows the extent of Philipse's holdings; the stars indicate the location of Philipse's Manor House at what is now Yonkers and at the Upper Mills in what is now North Tarrytown.

needful for the subsistence of man, except domestic cattle, which it would be easy to carry there; and besides producing many things of which our country is destitute.

A descendant of early Dutch pioneers on the Hudson, Franklin D. Roosevelt, commented on the homes and the persons who lived in them in these words:

We are prone to think of our forebears as living ideal lives of rural comfort in large houses with many rooms, with high ceilings and abundantly furnished, but one fact that stands out clearly. . . is that the mode of life of the first settlers of New Netherlands and of their immediate descendants was extremely simple, a statement which is true not only of the smaller landowners but of many of the patentees of large grants. From high to low their lives were the lives of pioneers, lives of hardship, or privation and often of danger. Roads were few and rough, household belongings modest, and the dwelling that contained more than four rooms was an exception.

In the mid-1700's, more than one farmer must have envied even a four-room house built of stone. For the great majority a cabin of rough-hewn wood still had to suffice. Like all pioneers, the families that lived in these crude dwellings labored long hours: the men working from sunrise to sundown in the fields in spring and summer, and calling on their wives to help with the autumn harvest. In the winter they turned to felling trees for timber, making barrel staves, and cutting wood for fireplaces. No matter how busy the wife might be with the children, she was expected to tend the house garden, watch over dried beans, corn, and fruit, pick berries, hunt for herbs, pickle or smoke meat for the long winter ahead, and make clothes of deerskin, linen, or knitted wool.

Virtually all the food was prepared over an open fire on the hearth, a back-breaking daily female chore. Iron kettles were heavy to handle, the roast on the spit had to be turned fre-

OPEN-HEARTH COOKING

This photograph of open-hearth cooking was taken in the kitchen of the restored Van Cortlandt Manor House. It shows a Dutch oven suspended over the fire, a spider pot heating milk over glowing embers, and bread rising in a pan atop a grill.

quently to avoid charring, and other dishes were cooked in long-handled spiders, on grills set beside the embers or in Dutch ovens—covered iron pots set in the coals with their lids also covered with coals. Bread was made in a beehive oven fashioned in the side wall of the fireplace. Burning coals were shoveled into the recess until it was hot, then the ashes were removed and the loaves of dough set on the hot bricks with a long wooden paddle called a peel. As children grew up they carried water from the well or nearby spring and helped sand wooden floors, or sweep them if they were of hard-packed earth. Hand-dipped candles were made from tallow recovered from butchering, but in poorer farmhouses cattails or rushes dipped in fat provided the meager illumination.

If this seems too arduous an existence, the coin had a shinier side. Everyone ate quite well after they had learned how to adapt to frontier life. The forests abounded in game, and the same fish the Mahicans had relished were still as abundant and the oysters just as plump. The Dutch *vrouwen* brought some of their old recipes across the Atlantic to the shores of the Hudson. A common dish was *erwten* or pea soup served most often with *olykoeks*, a roll that has been likened to doughnuts or bagels, and pumpkin bread, made from the vegetable the Indians showed them how to use. When the weather turned cool there was a dish called *hutspot* made by cooking carrots, onions, and potatoes together; and another dish, *rood kool*, spiced red cabbage. With such a plentiful diet, the Dutch settlers were typically wide of girth and round of face.

Hard-working folk know how to take advantage of leisure hours, and the early Dutch settlers were no exception. On Saturday evenings many of the men repaired to the taverns to spin tales, smoke their inordinately long pipes, and drink great quantities of spirits. There was plenty of local and imported beer, and the sugar or molasses for rum came in from the West Indies on almost every vessel. Bread and meat were washed down with various potions that bore names such as "Bride's Tears" and "Kill Devil." A report written shortly after the British takeover was to sum up local conditions thus:

32

NEW-YEAR'S DAY IN NEW AMSTERDAM IN OLD DUTCH TIMES

Among the holidays celebrated by those of Dutch extraction were *Kerstydt* (Christmas), *Nieuw Jaar* (New Year's Day), *Paas* (Easter), *Pinxter* (Whitsuntide), and *San Claas* (St. Nicholas Day), on December 5. This illustration, probably by Augustus Hoppin (1828–1896), was originally published in the January 1, 1859, issue of *Harper's Weekly*.

New York and Albany live wholly upon trade with the Indians, England and the West Indies. The returns for England are generally Beaver Peltry, Oile and Tobacco when we can have it. To the West Indies we send Flower, Bread, Pease, Pork and sometimes horses; the return from thence for the most part is Rumm, which pays the King a considerable excise, and some Molasses which serves the people to make drink and pays noe custom. There are about nine or ten three Mast Vessels of about eighty or a Hundred tons burthen, two or three ketches and Barks of about forty Tun, and about twenty Sloops of about twenty or five and twenty Tun belonging to the Government—All of which Trade for England, Holland and the West Indies, except five or six sloops that use the river Trade to Albany and that way.

In the early days, the Dutch Reformed Church was the state church, but not all of the inhabitants were devout parishioners. The first prominent minister was Dominie Everardus Bogardus, whose eloquent tongue was edged with steel. The good Dominie and the unpopular Director Willem Kieft quarreled constantly. When the pastor criticized the Director for his bad government, Kieft retorted that Bogardus preached in two ways, when "pretty drunk" and when "dead drunk." When Kieft charged that the minister became intoxicated after partaking of the Lord's Supper, he knew that the following Sabbath would be marked by a bitter sermon in retaliation. To prevent the Dominie's words from reaching too large an audience, Kieft sent the Fort Amsterdam Drum Corps to play loudly outside the church door and ordered the fort's guns to be fired at regular intervals. After years of suits and countersuits, the two men finally agreed to bury the hatchet and sailed together for Holland in 1647 on the *Princess*. But the boat was shipwrecked off the coast of England, and the two old foes drowned in the same angry surf.

These seafaring folk had a deep love of legends, tall tales, and hair-raising stories. Even Henry Hudson himself was not immune to the influence. As he had sailed up the Hudson beyond the Highlands, he noticed a point of land jutting out from the western shore above what is now Newburgh Bay. Through the slanting rays of sunshine, he made out a party of Indians, dancing around a campfire as if to welcome the approach of eventide. The earliest maps of the Hudson show this point as *Teufels' Danskammer* or the Devils' Ballroom, and it is generally believed that Hudson himself gave it that romantic name.

With such an early beginning, it was inevitable that legends would spring up and proliferate—like the strawberries which, some explorers reported, turned whole hillsides pink in the spring. While New Amsterdam was yet a small cluster of buildings, certain residents reported seeing a vessel moving easily against the ebb tide with all canvas set, making her way upriver. She answered no hails and disappeared into the evening mist. Rivermen claim they still catch glimpses of this American version of the *Flying Dutchman*, sails ballooned out even when there isn't a breath of wind, plowing the waters of the Hudson. She moves—in their words—through the narrow channel of the Highlands without tacking, defying tide and wind. If we are to believe these reports, the colors flying from her jackstaff are faded and nearly indistinguishable but nonetheless Dutch. It is futile to argue with those who have seen this eerie phenomenon, almost as futile as it is to tell other rivermen that Rambout Van Dam has stopped trying to make a landfall after three centuries of penance on the lower reaches of the Hudson.

Van Dam was a gay young blade who lived on Spuyten Duyvil near today's Baker Field (of Columbia University) and nothing could deter him if he knew of a place where there was drinking and dancing. Hearing of a party planned for a farmhouse near present-day Nyack, Rambout put on his best clothes and rowed up the river, past the Palisades, into the Tappan Zee, and thence to the landing place near the farm. It was a Saturday evening and everyone was enjoying himself when the big kitchen clock tolled out the hour of midnight. Rambout's hosts, devout Dutchmen, ordered the roistering stopped. More than a little tipsy, Van Dam staggered down to where his boat was tied to a willow root. His friends warned him that it was already the Sabbath and that he should not travel on the day set aside for rest and prayer. "I'll not land until I reach Spuyten Duyvil," he roared, jumping into the boat and grasping the oars. Those were the last words of poor Rambout Van Dam. Rivermen on the Tappan Zee say he has not reached home yet, and many a fisherman or steamboat pilot has sworn that he has seen the shadowy form of the oarsman rowing for the shore.

These two legends are familiar only on the Hudson, but there are others known all around the world, thanks above all to the literary artistry of Washington Irving (1783–1859). Born in New York City, Irving loved the river all his life. While still a relatively young man, he heard of legendary characters whose exploits he could fictionally relate to the Hudson. He wrote *The Legend of Sleepy Hollow* and *Rip Van Winkle*, two stories that for generations have delighted children and adults alike.

The first deals with lonely Ichabod Crane, a Yankee schoolteacher who fell head over heels in love with plump, seductive Katrina Van Tassel, whose rich father's farm abutted the river on the east bank near Tarrytown. Unfortunately, the young maiden was courted and admired by one Brom Bones, a burly bully who had no liking for the Yankee teacher. One night after a merry dinner and dance at the Van Tassel home, Ichabod, rejected and dejected, left for home astride a sorry horse that was all skin and bones. Riding through the deep forest near the Pocantico River, the teacher suddenly heard the pounding of hoofbeats coming up fast behind him. He turned and beheld a specter, a headless horseman clad in a flowing garment like a sheet. Feverishly, Ichabod spurred his feeble mount, but it was in vain. At the bridge over the lesser stream, just above where Frederick Philipse had built a church some years before, the specter rose in his stirrups and hurled his head at the terror-stricken schoolmaster. Nothing was ever seen of Crane again, but on the bank of the Pocantico searchers found a shattered pumpkin and Ichabod's ancient stovepipe hat.

The story of Rip Van Winkle is set in the 1760s—the period around the end of the English regime and the beginnings of the

THE HEADLESS HORSEMAN PURSUES ICHABOD CRANE

In the climactic scene from *The Legend of Sleepy Hollow,* by
Washington Irving, Ichabod Crane strives vainly to escape the
pursuit of the dreaded Headless Horseman. This illustration is
one of six for *The Legend of Sleepy Hollow* drawn by Felix O. C.
Darley and published in 1849 by the American Art Union.

American Revolution. A hen-pecked husband, good-natured but somewhat bibulous, Rip wandered away from his native village and wound up in the high hills and hidden glens of the Catskills. There he heard a sound as of distant thunder and, when he investigated, discovered a band of little men playing at bowls. They let him play with them and offered him great draughts from a supply of liquor they were sampling. Twenty years later, Rip awoke from his liquor-induced sleep to find his clothes in tatters, his fowling piece rotted and rusted, and his faithful dog gone. No one in his home town recognized him; his cronies were long since dead. The astonishing changes time had wrought taxed his sanity. So, today, when summer storms sweep out of the hills toward the Hudson, with lightning flashing and thunder booming in reverberating crescendos, residents look knowingly at one another and say that Rip's little men are still bowling in some hidden glen high in the mountains.

With these two marvelous legends, Washington Irving made that portion of the river near the Tappan Zee famous as Sleepy Hollow, a name neither the years nor the fast-moving changes of the nineteenth and twentieth centuries could erase. Irving had spent his young years in Manhattan where, according to family legend, on an auspicious day at the time of the inauguration of America's first President, George Washington patted him on the head when his nurse told the General the boy was named for him.

Still young, Irving made a trip up the Hudson with an older relative on board a sloop bound for Albany. Years later, he wrote of this first glimpse of the Hudson's grandeur in words that no modern travel writer has surpassed. One paragraph is enough to show how impressed the future man of letters was:

> What a time of intense delight was that first sail through the Highlands. I sat on the deck as we slowly tided along at the foot of those stern mountains, and gazed with wonder and admiration at cliffs impending far above me, crowned with forests, with eagles sailing and screaming around them; or listened to the unseen stream dashing down precipices; or

RIP VAN WINKLE

This painting of Rip Van Winkle asleep in the Catskill Mountains
is by A. D. O. Browere (1814–1887), who lived most of his life in
the Hudson Valley.

WASHINGTON IRVING WITH GEORGE WASHINGTON

It is said that in 1789, when Washington Irving was 6 years old, his Scottish nurse presented the boy to his namesake, George Washington, who offered his blessing. The event was commemorated in a poem, "Chieftain and Child," by William W. Waldron, and in a watercolor painting done at age 15 by George B. Butler, who later became a known American portrait and genre artist. Butler gave the painting to his friend Waldron, who in turn gave it to Washington Irving, who hung it at Sunnyside, his home in Tarrytown, New York, where it has hung ever since.

beheld rock, and tree, and cloud, and sky reflected in the glassy stream of the river. And then how solemn and thrilling the scene as we anchored at night at the foot of those mountains, clothed with overhanging forests; and everything grew dark and mysterious; and I heard the plaintive note of the whippoorwill from the mountain-side, or was startled now and then by the sudden leap and heavy splash of the sturgeon.

Irving's description of the Hudson Valley followed a long pattern of laudatory reports which from the first had led many Europeans to seek a new life for themselves in the New World. The population grew apace in New Netherland and later New York, although never as fast as in New England. Germans from the Palatine settled up the river near Rhinebeck to work at getting turpentine, tar, and other naval stores from the pine forests. When this industry fell on slow days, many of the Germans moved to the west side of the river.

French Huguenots, driven out of their homeland by the Catholic King of France, passed through the Dutch towns on the lower river and found a small valley to their liking a short distance inland. There they built a row of stone houses in a town called New Paltz—stout little fortresses strung like beads along a single strand. How could they know, these dozen or so families, that those stone residences would survive the centuries so well that even today they look much as they did long before the American Revolution? The site they occupy has been called the oldest intact street in the United States and fully deserves its reputation.

Many Dutch, German, and Huguenot settlers prospered along the river, thereby confirming the predictions of one traveler after another. As early as 1670, Daniel Denton published what modern real estate agents would call a glowing prospectus, parts of which describe in detail the way colonists took up their land:

. . . the usual way is for a Company to joyn together either enough to make a Town, or a lesser number; These go. . . to view a tract of land, there being choice enough, and finding a place convenient for a town, they return to the Governor. . . who gives them a Grant or Patent for the said land. For the manner how they get a livelihood, it is principally by Corn & Cattel, which will there fetch them any Commodities; likewise they sowe stores of Flax which they make every one Cloth for their own wearing, as also woolen cloth, and Linsey-Woolsey, & had they more Tradesmen among them they would in a little time live without the help of any other Country for their Clothing; For Tradesmen there is none but live happily there, as Carpenters, Blacksmiths, Masons, Tailors, Weavers, Shoemakers, Tanners, Brickmakers, & so any other Trade; them that have no Trade betake themselves to Husbandry, get land of their own and live exceeding well.

In 1643 Father Isaac Jogues, the Jesuit missionary who was subsequently martyred and then canonized, wrote that Manhattan Island was populated by more than a score of different nationalities who spoke at least eighteen different languages. The usual time for a voyage outbound from Holland or the Channel Coast of France was seven or eight weeks but, with the prevailing westerlies in their favor, ships went back across the Atlantic in a month or five weeks. This did not mean that settlers could expect to reach the New World that easily. Ships had to avoid storms, wait for propitious winds, and spend long periods of time in port loading and unloading cargo. They were also confronted with the possibility of a pirate attack at sea. Nevertheless, the vaunted attractions of the Hudson Valley continued to lure more and more settlers—ultimately to become New Yorkers.

CROW-NEST FROM BULL HILL, ON THE HUDSON RIVER

Typical of many splendid views along the Hudson River is this scene captured
by W. H. Bartlett (1809–1854), originally published in London in 1839.

Sleepy Hollow Restorations

Chapter III

The English Take Over

How successful were the Dutch in settling along the Hudson? For decades they had more tangible advantages and benefits than any other people settling the New World. The climate was not too cold for agriculture nor so warm that it bred indolence. Life in the Netherlands during the Dutch "golden age" of expansion was more advanced and freer than anywhere else on earth. Yet the bounties that the Hudson offered could not offset the mistakes and miscalculations of the men in the counting houses back home.

Between the periods of leadership of Peter Minuit and Peter Stuyvesant lay a barren stretch during which the new colony was governed by mediocre men. Stubborn, thick-headed, narrow, venal, and weak, these administrators let a golden opportunity slip through their fingers. By the time Stuyvesant was transferred from Curaçao to New Amsterdam in 1647, the damage was done. The tenuous early friendship between the red man and the white man was dissipated in a succession of land manipulations by rapacious land grabbers. To do him justice, the peg-legged Stuyvesant tried to do what he could, but the task was too great. There was physical danger on every frontier, and moral decay at the center of power.

In 1650, Adrian Van der Donck, the first historian of the colony, was writing that the fort that sheltered the main settlement "lies like a mole-heap or a tottering wall, on which there is

The English Take Over

not one gun carriage or one piece of cannon in a suitable frame or on a good platform." Van der Donck minced no words: "In our opinion this country will never flourish under the government of the Honorable [Dutch West India] Company," he wrote a friend, "but will pass away and come to an end of itself." The year that letter was penned, Stuyvesant was forced to swallow his pride and sign a treaty giving the English the eastern half of Long Island and most of the land west of the Connecticut River. The most he could salvage was an agreement that the New Englanders would not settle within ten miles of the Hudson. Despite the Dutch claim to the Delaware (South River), Sweden established a colony near present-day Wilmington in defiance of the Honorable Company and the States-General.

Irony played its part in this drama of rivalry on the Delaware. The leader of the Swedes was none other than Peter Minuit, the founding father of New Amsterdam. Recalled from the burgeoning little settlement at the mouth of the Hudson because the Company felt he had failed to squeeze large enough profits out of the fur trade, Minuit looked elsewhere for recognition. Finding employment in Sweden, he led a group of Swedes and Finns in the establishment of Fort Christina, named for the young Swedish Queen. For eighteen years the tiny Swedish enclave in the New World was a bother to the Dutch. Then in 1655, Stuyvesant sent a fleet of seven ships with 650 soldiers to halt the intruders.

The encroachment of the Swedes had been stopped, but the onrush of Englishmen continued apace. Up the Hudson, the tenuous peace with the Indians was deteriorating. Cheated by the settlers around the mouth of the Esopus, the Indians retaliated with firebrand and tomahawk, spreading terror throughout the Dutch holdings on the west bank. Stuyvesant sent troops to support the towns and then spent many a day shuttling back and forth by sloop between Esopus and New Amsterdam trying to establish peace, finally attained only in 1660, with the Peace of Esopus.

The end of Dutch dominion came four years later. Charles II of England, badly in need of cash, and desirous of ridding Eng-

PETER STUYVESANT

Arriving in New Amsterdam in 1647, Peter Stuyvesant
(1592–1672), became the last Dutch Governor in the colony,
serving until its surrender to the English in 1664. This portrait is
in oil on a wooden panel, painted from life by an unidentified
artist.

land of Dutch commercial rivalry, decided to push the Dutch out of the New World. This was accomplished by his invoking the claims to the Atlantic coastal region asserted by John Cabot in the 1490s. The King called in his brother, the Duke of York, spread out a map of North America, and circled the area held by the Dutch. He bestowed this territory on the Duke prior to his sending a well-equipped fleet of men-of-war to oust the "usurpers." Under the command of Colonel Richard Nicolls, the English fleet dropped anchor off the tip of Manhattan and trained its broadsides at the worm-eaten, wooden palisades of Fort Amsterdam. Nicolls demanded unconditional surrender, but he was astute enough to promise the residents equal rights with Englishmen if they swore allegiance to the British crown. The choleric Stuyvesant, stomping around on his silver-encrusted peg leg, assembled a hasty meeting of his councillors in the upper rooms of Willem Kieft's old tavern, converted into the city hall. Passionately he called on the people to resist. But his listeners, gazing out of the windows, saw first the powerful British warships riding at anchor and then the rusty Dutch cannon on the rotting ramparts of the fort. No one wanted to fight.

On a pleasant late summer morning—September 8, 1664 —Nicolls sent his troops ashore to accept the Dutch surrender. Not a shot was fired. Dutch control had lasted for only fifty-five years. Some nine years later, there still appeared to be a spark of life in the Dutch empire on the mainland of North America. During one of the innumerable wars between Holland and England in the latter part of the seventeenth century, a Dutch fleet recaptured the port that had become New York, again without the need to fire a single gun. But the incident remained isolated and ineffectual. The Treaty of Westminster, in 1674, ending the war, returned the Dutch holdings to the English by the end of the next year. This time the Hudson would stay in British hands until the people of New York and its sister colonies took the road of national independence.

It is difficult to imagine a transition from one ruling power to another that went more smoothly than the one in New York. By wise design, the new English rulers left intact almost all the

NEW AMSTERDAM, C. 1673

In 1664, The Dutch surrendered New Amsterdam to the English, who renamed it New York. Although the Dutch briefly took control of the port again in 1673, the Treaty of Westminster of 1674 returned it to the English by the end of the next year. This view of New Amsterdam c. 1763 is from a copper engraving by Peter Schenk, first issued c. 1702.

49

The English Take Over

institutions in the colony. Dutchmen went through the formality of swearing new allegiance to the British crown and found little to worry about. Men like Frederick Philipse and Stephanus Van Cortlandt enhanced their commercial activities under the new flag. Within a few years their previous holdings were recognized and expanded upon by the English. Along with other prominent individuals, they were given high office in government.

Ordinary citizens also profited from the changeover. They retained freedom of worship in the church of their choice, and enjoyed equal esteem with all the other residents—a condition more tolerant than that existing in England itself at the time. Basic conditions for earning one's livelihood changed little if at all. So, not surprisingly, the Dutch culture prevailed for years and can still be detected along the Hudson. It survived in numerous words which the English adopted, in dishes the newcomers found agreeable to their taste, and in the love of well-built, stout houses. As long as the inhabitants relied on wind to propel their boats, the Dutch sloop reigned supreme on the Hudson.

Nowhere is the transition from Dutch to English rule so dramatically illustrated as in the careers of the men who founded and developed the holdings known as Philipsburg Manor. Frederick Philipse, as noted previously, had started his career in North America as a carpenter for the West India Company. Through two advantageous marriages and his own business acumen, he built up his landholdings until, at his death, he owned two hundred square miles of land. Serving as city councilman in New Amsterdam, he traded in furs, grain, and flour, wines and brandies, tobacco, horses, lumber, molasses, rum, and slaves. When the English took over, Philipse faced no obstacles to further land purchases. In fact, the English system of establishing grants to manors helped him to amass larger acreage. In the belief that support of large landholdings would maintain the status quo and create a class of conservative landlords who would help the Crown, England created a system of landholding proprietors in the Middle Colonies of New York, New Jersey, and Pennsylvania.

The English Take Over

Near the mouth of the Pocantico River, Frederick Philipse built a stone house and office, a grist mill, a cooperage, a bakeshop for making ship's biscuits, and a wharf at which sloops could tie up. This became part of an overall scheme to develop and use his Manor holdings, which included other mills and farmlands in the area of today's Yonkers. It was undoubtedly the first industrial-commercial complex in the colony.

Although his political and business obligations kept him in town most of the time, Philipse frequently visited his development on the Pocantico. He built the stone Dutch Reformed Church nearby that still stands. In the fields back from the river his tenants raised grain to be ground at his mill. In the forests, trees were felled for making barrels, and for sale as cut and trimmed lumber. Gardens were tilled and meat cured for the winter. Frederick left his holdings to his son Adolph. Just as shrewd a businessman as his father, the latter also served at one time or another as a member of the King's Council, a judge of the Supreme Court, a Representative in the Assembly and a Speaker of that body, holding the last post for twenty years. The population of the Manor grew from two hundred in 1702 when Frederick died to eleven hundred in 1750 when Adolph died.

During these years, the Indian population continued to decrease, largely because the natives left the built-up areas and went deeper into the wilderness as European civilization encroached upon them. Not all of them went away, however: records and letters reveal that some became squatters, setting their homes at the edge of a field not too far from the white habitations and eking out a meager existence by bringing in game for the table and doing other odd jobs. With periodic warfare breaking out between the French and the English along with their Indian allies, the more sedentary Indians bowed to the white man's superiority in firearms and also retreated further inland. Some of the tribesmen went west while others moved south or joined other local tribes.

By intermarriage the prominent manorial families kept power in their own hands without diffusing it. As the eighteenth century dawned, it seemed as if all the Philipses, Van

PHILIPSBURG MANOR, UPPER MILLS

The gristmill and wharf built by Frederick Philipse were an important part of the industrial-commercial complex at Philipsburg Manor Upper Mills. The reconstructed mill and dock and nearby manor house are now maintained by Sleepy Hollow Restorations. This recent illustration by Robert Fink recreates the scene much as it would have appeared during Philipse's lifetime.

OLD DUTCH CHURCH, NORTH TARRYTOWN

A stone Dutch Reformed Church was built by Frederick
Philipse near his manor house and trading center in what is now
North Tarrytown. The Old Dutch Church still stands, and
buried in its adjacent graveyard is the author Washington Irving.
This illustration is by Edgar M. Bacon (1855–1935), artist and
author of *Chronicles of Tarrytown and Sleepy Hollow* and
The Hudson River—From Ocean to Source (1902).

ADOLPH PHILIPSE

Portrait of Adolph Philipse (1665–1750), second owner of
Philipsburg Manor, in oil on pine panel, c. 1695, by an unknown
artist.

The English Take Over

Cortlandts, Livingstons, De Lanceys, Schuylers, and Van Rensselaers were cousins or in-laws. Certain perquisites had a way of falling invariably into the laps of the big landowners. Frederick Philipse, for instance, when accorded the royal grant for his holdings including the land near Spuyten Duyvil, was authorized to build and maintain a bridge across the river separating Manhattan from the mainland and to charge a toll for man, beast, and wagon. He had to let the King's soldiers pass free but this was no great loss of revenue. The Van Cortlandts were granted the right to operate a ferry across the Croton River and maintain a tavern for housing and feeding travelers.

In May, 1748, Pierre Van Cortlandt married Joanna Livingston, tying two famous families even more tightly together. As mistress of the house, Joanna not only bore eight children, but managed a large number of servants, oversaw the preparation of food by the cooks, the curing and storing of meats, fruits, vegetables, and other supplies, and, according to family tradition, still had time to design the "long walk" that led from the house to the tavern and ferry landing.

Along this walk were gardens filled with blooms, some native and some imported from Holland. Her guest list read like a colonial *Who's Who*: Governors Tryon and Clinton and Benjamin Franklin were among the many notables who enjoyed the gracious hospitality of the manor house.

The same was true at the other big homes. In his book, *In the Valley*, Harold Frederic described an evening at the Van Rensselaers' Albany mansion:

> You may still see for yourselves how noble, one might say palatial, was the home which young Stephen Van Rensselaer built for himself, there on the lowlands at the end of Broadway, across from Kissing Bridge. But no power of fancy can restore for you . . . the flashing glories of that spectacle: the broad, fine front of the Manor House, with all its windows blazing in welcome; the tall trees in front aglow with swinging lanterns and colored lights, hung cunningly in their shadowy branches after some Italian device; the

PIERRE VAN CORTLANDT

Portrait of Pierre Van Cortlandt (1721–1814), first Lieutenant Governor of New York State, oil on canvas by John Wesley Jarvis (1780–1840).

JOANNA LIVINGSTON VAN CORTLANDT

Portrait of Joanna Livingston Van Cortlandt (1722–1808), wife of
Pierre Van Cortlandt. The portrait has been said to have been
painted from life c. 1792 by Ezra Ames (1768–1836), but other
art historians suggest that it was painted posthumously, c. 1812,
by an unknown artist, from a wax miniature profile of the
subject.

stately carriages sweeping up the gravelled avenue, and discharging their passengers at the block; the gay procession up the wide stone steps—rich velvets and costly satins, powdered wigs and alabaster throats, bright eyes, and gems on swordhilts or at fair breasts—all radiant in the hospitable flood of light streaming from the open door; the throng of gaping slaves with torches, and smartly dressed servants holding the horses or helping with my lady's train and cloak.

Frederic's prose may sound extravagant, but life in the manor houses was very comfortable for the wealthy. Moreover, those early patricians possessed an eye for scenic beauty. Their homes, for the most part, rested on pleasant eminences beside the Hudson where the view up and down the river was breathtaking.

The Marquis de Chastellux, third in command of the French expeditionary army that came across the Atlantic to help the American patriots in the War of Independence, traveled along the Hudson on several occasions when he was not on army duty. Once he came upon the scene at West Point and in his journal, called *Travels in North America, in the Years* 1780–81–82, he described the view in these words:

You at length take advantage of a spot where the mountains are a bit less high to turn to the westward and approach the river, but you still cannot see it. Descending slowly, at a turn of the road, my eyes were suddenly struck with the most magnificent picture I have ever beheld. It was a view of the North [Hudson] River, running in a deep channel formed by the mountains, through which in former ages it had forced its passage.

On another occasion the Marquis, a man of vast culture, an Encyclopedist and member of the French Academy who was no stranger to travel and far places, visited Wappinger Falls, Glens Falls, and the cataract at Cohoes, each one eliciting his praise for its beauty. The Marquis was not only a brave ally in war; he was a champion of the Hudson River and its beauty, and punctuated the pages of his diary with words of praise for it.

Garmented in beauty, the river was no less attractive to the hard-working ordinary men and women who did not live in ease or luxury. When they could, they built their simple homes beside the stream or on the slopes of the mountains where the view was as fine as from the mansion of the Lord of the Manor. Like the Indians, these farmers and artisans feasted on the oysters dug from the tidal flats or on the shad caught in nets strung halfway across the stream. Those of Dutch extraction celebrated five holidays, *Kerstydt* (Christmas), *Nieuw Jaar* (New Year's Day), *Paas* (Easter), *Pinxter* (Whitsuntide), and *San Claas* (St. Nicholas Day) on December 5. On those festive occasions, they ate what they had eaten in their homeland, but with local variations: *suppawn and malk* (corn mush and milk), *hoof kaas* (head cheese), *kool slaa* (cole slaw), and *zult* (sausage), as well as native dishes such as pumpkin pie, fish chowder, and a kind of shepherd's pie.

Germans, Huguenots, Walloons, Englishmen, and a dozen other nationalities swapped recipes, helped each other at house and barn raisings, played together, and often prayed together because of necessity. For a long time, when they went from place to place on business, for parties or a-courting, they traveled by boat. The Hudson was a tie that bound them together. Just before and after the Revolutionary War, it was even the preferred travel route for many who lived in western Connecticut. Making their way through the Litchfield and Taconic hills to the river, they sailed down to New York by a sloop rather than suffer the vagaries and hardships of traveling all the way by road.

This idyllic scene was invaded and transformed in the 1760s and the 1770s by developments that could not be denied: the Sugar Act, the Stamp Act, restrictions on colonial trade, and the quartering of red-coated soldiers in private homes in New York City. The policies of the mother country sharpened tensions as a yeasty ferment grew in the hearts of many in the New

World. Men and women who had overcome bad weather, hunger, disease, loneliness, and hostile Indians with almost no help from the other side of the Atlantic found that they had become independent in spirit if not in fact. Many of their neighbors who had undergone the same trials, however, still clung to the traditional beliefs and ideals. Now neighbor looked with growing suspicion on neighbor as the chasm between patriot and Tory grew wider and deeper. Liberty poles went up in village squares and city streets; Sons of Liberty trained with pitchforks and squirrel guns.

Everywhere in the valley there was dissension. Frederick Philipse III, great-grandson of the founder of Philipsburg Manor, opted for the British Crown. His neighbor to the north, Pierre Van Cortlandt, chose the patriot cause. Family ties were torn asunder at every social level. The British Governor, William Tryon, sought to fan the fires of dissension, hoping to keep New York from supporting the more militant leaders of rebellion in New England and Virginia. One day, in 1774, thinking to win over Pierre Van Cortlandt, the Governor called for his sloop and sailed upriver to Croton Point, accompanied by his wife and several aides. Courteous but aloof, the Van Cortlandts welcomed the party and put them up for the night. After breakfast the next morning, the Governor and his military aide proposed to their host that they take a stroll to the top of a high hill behind the house. The view of the Hudson was magnificent, but Tryon had not come to enjoy the scenery. He quickly came to the point of his visit, proposing that if the head of the family stayed loyal to the Crown there would naturally be benefits for him, including handsome grants of land and, perhaps, even a title. Here it is useful to listen to the account written by Pierre's son, Phillip:

> My father then observed that he was chosen a representative by unanimous approbation of a people who placed confidence in his integrity to use all his ability for their benefit and the good of his country as a true patriot which line of conduct he was determined to pursue.

Philip added that the Governor's party took "a short and

PORTRAIT SAID TO BE OF FREDERICK PHILIPSE III

John Wollaston the Younger, an English artist, painted this
portrait, which is believed to be of Frederick Philipse III.
During the American Revolution, Philipse supported the British
cause. He fled to Great Britain after the war, and his lands were
confiscated and sold at public auction.

hasty farewell, and embarked upon the sloop and returned to New York." Philip himself took off his insignia as a major in Tryon's Guards and a short time later was made a lieutenant colonel in a New York regiment authorized by the Continental Congress.

Chapter IV

The War of Independence

Patriotic New Yorkers went into the Revolution suffering from many illusions. True, they had seen their own Liberty Boys, disguised as Indians, dump tea in the harbor just as others had done at Boston, and late in the summer after the British defeat in Boston a British ship lobbed shells into the city. Less than four days after the enemy fleet sailed out of Boston harbor, George Washington sent General William Heath with five regiments of foot and two companies of artillery down the Post Road toward New York, soon followed by the balance of the American forces.

There was never any real doubt in the mind of the commander in chief about New York's strategic importance. He sensed that the British would want the excellent harbor as an anchorage for their huge armada. With a large force stationed in Canada another army could be sent to the mouth of the Hudson to undertake a pincers movement that would cut the colonies in two. It therefore became a matter of urgency for the patriots to build defenses, and, as one writer put it, "they dug like prairie dogs." Batteries were placed at the tip of Manhattan and across the Hudson at Paulus Hook. Forts were built at the upper end of Manhattan (Fort Washington) and across the river (Fort Lee). Other redoubts were scattered about the island's perimeter to forestall a seaborne invasion.

As all this occurred, the British force grew apace. The

blockading squadron was strengthened when General Sir William Howe brought an army down from Halifax. By June 30, 1776, there were 130 enemy ships in the Lower Bay. Two weeks later, Admiral Lord Richard Howe, the general's brother, arrived with 150 more ships filled with troops. Then in succession came German mercenaries, more British soldiers from England, and finally Cornwallis's expeditionary force from Charleston, South Carolina. All in all, the British had 31, 625 men encamped on Staten Island. To support them, there were ten ships of the line, twenty frigates, and scores of other vessels mounting twelve hundred guns in all. It was the largest expeditionary force England had ever sent overseas. With such formidable naval power, it was easy to land troops on Long Island before the Battle of Brooklyn, an American defeat.

Washington fell back to the heights of upper Manhattan and, as if to show that the revolutionary spirit was still very much alive, fought off the British at the battle of Harlem Heights where the campus of Columbia University is now located. For a time, the Hudson became the focal point of the war. The patriots, hoping to deny the river to the enemy fleet, had built an obstruction of sunken ships and pointed timbers between Forts Washington and Lee. But two British frigates, the *Phoenix* and the *Rose*, defied the batteries at the forts, rode over the man-made obstacle on a flood tide, and spent the next few weeks harassing residents from the Tappan Zee.

The response was not long in coming. On a warm August night, determined American soldiers and rivermen gathered together a tiny flotilla of small boats and attempted to set the British frigates afire. They were easily driven off, but the two enemy ships soon sailed down to rejoin the vast armada in New York Bay. While Washington was pondering how to defend the Hudson corridor, the city of New York was nearly burned down. No one ever determined whether the blaze was set by foolish patriots or drunken British soldiers, but the conflagration did not make life any pleasanter for the occupying enemy during the winters they held the city.

After the Battle of White Plains, the British were able to

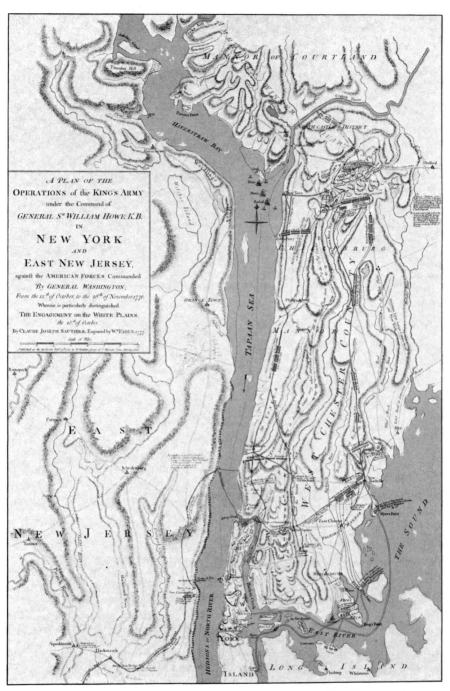

Sleepy Hollow Restorations

THE *Howe Map* OF THE BATTLE OF WHITE PLAINS

The map on page 65 shows the Plan of the Operation of the King's Army under the Command of General Sir William Howe, K.B. in New York and East New Jersey, against the American Forces Commanded by General Washington, at the time of the Battle of White Plains. The *Howe Map,* as it is called, was originally drawn by Claude Joseph Sauthier and engraved in England by William Faden in 1777. A facsimile edition of the map is published by Sleepy Hollow Restorations.

capture Fort Washington and then Fort Lee and gain safe access to the lower thirty-five miles of the Hudson. It was a hazardous period for the towns along that stretch of the river. English craft now cruised the Tappan Zee at will, sent small boats ashore to steal food, harass the natives, and impress men for their "row-galleys."

When the main course of the war shifted to New Jersey and the Delaware River, a degree of peace returned to the Hudson except for hit-and-run raids in the "Neutral Ground," the contemporary term used to describe the no-man's-land in Westchester County on the east bank of the Hudson. Away to the north, the first strong effort of the British to start down the Lake Champlain—Hudson corridor was thwarted by Benedict Arnold and his hastily thrown-together "navy" at the Battle of Valcour Island. Arnold was defeated, but he delayed the invasion for a year.

Meanwhile the American forces were fortifying the approaches to the Highlands, knowing that topography would aid them in preventing the enemy from coming upriver. At Stony Point, on the west bank of the Hudson, a crude fort was erected. Across the stream at Verplanck's Point, a small fort protected King's Ferry, now the nearest safe crossing to New York City and a vital link between New England and the rest of the country.

By the summer of 1777, the British were ready to make a major attempt to cut the young nation in two. Sir Henry Clinton moved north on the Hudson with a small fleet of warships and transports after General John ("Gentleman Johnny") Burgoyne, who had won King George's approval for the grand design of the campaign, moved south out of Canada. At first, all went smoothly for Burgoyne. He moved his train and guns down Lake Champlain by boat, overcame spotty resistance, and seized Fort Ticonderoga, the supposedly impregnable lock on the Americans' northern gate. His imposing army consisted of thousands of British regulars, Hessian and Brunswick mercenaries, and scores of Indians. There was a sharp skirmish at Hubbardton, where the American militia was overwhelmed in two hours.

Then Burgoyne planned a foraging raid into Vermont to win Tory support and to gather horses that were badly needed. His Brunswick dragoons, all dressed in heavy uniforms, with boots and spurs, had no mounts and were ordered to bring in meat on the hoof. To command this force, he named Lieutenant Colonel Frederick Baum, a German who could not speak a word of English.

But he had reckoned without John Stark and his New Hampshire militia. Stark, with two thousand men, moved out from Bennington and waited for the enemy on the Walloomsac River, a stream that is actually in New York State. Irascible, temperamental, and often at odds with his superiors, John Stark was nonetheless a good tactician. He made his first move against Baum by sending strong flanks out to encircle the enemy. There was bitter fighting in the deep woods along the river, the sort of fighting the Green Mountain Boys loved best. The German soldiers were picked off one by one and their allied Indians and Tories, seeing this, melted away to the rear. Baum held out until Lieutenant Colonel Heinrich Breymann came on with seven hundred more men, but they too were unable to shift from parade-ground maneuvering to oppose the open-order fighting style of the Americans.

When dusk fell, the weary, beaten Germans staggered back along the road they had come, leaving four cannon, hundreds of rifles, muskets, and broadswords in the corpse-strewn woods behind them. It was a victory the militia would never forget, for it meant that with able leadership these raw troops could give a good accounting of themselves. For Burgoyne, it was the beginning of the end. He waited at Skenesboro for a second force under Barry St. Leger to come down the Mohawk and join him. But a New York militia general named Nicholas Herkimer, stubborn and fearless, confronted St. Leger at Oriskany, defeated him and sent his force fleeing back to Canada.

Worried now, Gentleman Johnny wrote Sir Henry Clinton in New York City, urgently requesting the latter to begin a diversionary attack up the Hudson. Clinton was slow to move. He waited for reinforcements to arrive from the home country and then planned little more than a feint upriver, rather than a full-fledged rush to Burgoyne's rescue. To illustrate the lack of coordination of command, an order for Sir Henry to move lay untouched for days in a desk drawer of the Colonial Secretary in London, while the latter was off on a fox hunt.

Finally, driven as much by fear of hunger as a conviction that he could alter the course of events by fighting, the British commander sent his men across the Hudson on September 13 on a bridge of rafts. Five days later, General Benjamin Lincoln with New England militia moved in behind the British and cut their links to the forces on Lake Champlain. For the patriots along the Hudson, it was nevertheless an hour of great concern. To them it seemed Burgoyne had advanced swiftly and easily. But New Yorkers who adhered to the British cause thought this was good news. More numerous in New York than in any other state, the Tories had regularly attempted to undermine the patriot cause. Now, they thought, relief was in sight.

All though this period, the New Yorkers created a new government and mobolized for a long war. George Clinton took office in 1777 as first Governor of New York, with Pierre Van Cortlandt his Lieutenant Governor. Pierre's son, young Philip Van Cortlandt of the 2nd New York Continental Regiment was ordered to help stop St. Leger, but was then shifted to the forces facing Burgoyne. In that regiment, sons of prominent landowners, tenant farmers, wheelwrights, servants, and clerks from the lower Hudson marched shoulder to shoulder. Untrained the army may have been, but it was motivated by a common purpose.

Far upriver, below Saratoga, Burgoyne marshalled his forces for a battle against General Horatio Gates, still hoping for Sir Henry Clinton to create a diversion, but realizing that his best hope of success was a breakthrough to Albany. Had he known that Thaddeus Kosciuszko, the freedom-loving Polish general, had selected the battlefield and supervised the preparation of positions, Gentleman Johnny might have been less sanguine.

GOVERNOR GEORGE CLINTON

George Clinton took office in 1777 as the first Governor of New York; Pierre Van Cortlandt served as his Lieutenant Governor. This American School portrait of Clinton is owned by the Historical Society of the Tarrytowns.

The War of Independence

The morning of September 19, 1777, broke clear, crisp, and cool, as the British moved out of their camp on the Hudson shore to strike at the Americans on Bemis Heights. Burgoyne had planned a three-pronged attack: Fraser on the right to turn the American left, Hamilton in the center with more Britishers, and Baron Von Reidesel, commander of the Hessians and Brunswickers, heading down the river road. Gates planned a wise defense, making use of Kosciuszko's entrenchments. On his left was Benedict Arnold with Daniel Morgan's riflemen from the Carolinas. In the center were Learned's men from Massachusetts and the 4th New York under James Livingston. Nearest the river was Gates with John Glover's Marblehead Brigade and those of John Paterson and John Nixon from Massachusetts.

These forces met in a clearing called Freeman's Farm and fought almost an entire day in a bloody, seesaw conflict. Arnold led his forces with vigor and courage, damaging the British center badly. Morgan's sharpshooters did great damage, not the least being the silencing of the big enemy guns. The Carolinian backwoodsmen were so accurate with their Pennsylvania-made rifles that the British gunners could not serve their cannon. Many mistakes were made by the British, who fought without cohesion, and only the timely arrival of the Germans under battle-wise Von Reidesel from the river road saved the redcoats from a worse trouncing.

The first day of the Battle of Saratoga was disappointing to both sides. Burgoyne, who had not broken through, had suffered heavy losses. Some military theorists hold that because Gates would not accede to Arnold's demand for more men to break through the enemy's center, a feat which Arnold nearly accomplished nonetheless with fragments of several regiments, Gates lost the opportunity to annihilate the foe. Burgoyne ordered entrenchments dug, and settled down on Freeman's Farm to wait for word of succor from the south. Two days later it arrived. A courier brought word that Sir Henry Clinton was at last moving up the river. The battle for the Hudson corridor shifted with dramatic speed to the Highlands, leaving the

71

BENEDICT ARNOLD

Although he commanded American troops courageously and
successfully during the early years of the war, Benedict Arnold is
best remembered for his attempt to turn West Point over to the
British, and his name has become synonymous with "traitor."
This steel engraving of Arnold was originally published in New
York in 1859, in the volume of *Illustrations to Irving's Life of
Washington.*

72

bloodied and battered troops at Saratoga resting on their arms.

Sir Henry possessed excellent information about the patriots' situation. The Tories of the valley had had plenty of time to spy out the section and send maps and troop dispositions. These reports showed the existence of a small group of weak forts, manned by raw troops in insufficient numbers. Near Dunderberg Mountain on the west side of the river was Popolopen Creek with Forts Clinton and Montgomery nearby. Across the Hudson was half-completed Fort Independence, near Anthony's Nose. Clintons were in command on both sides: Sir Henry Clinton's American opponents in the fortifications on the west bank were led by Brigadier General George Clinton, the fighting governor of New York State, and his brother, Brigadier General James Clinton. In the hills of what is now Putnam County lay General Israel Putnam's force of untrained militia and a few regulars, plus a company of Lamb's Continental artillery.

Sir Henry, privy to the true situation in the enemy camp, moved with decisive speed. He feinted toward the east bank but put his main force ashore in a dense fog near Stony Point on the west shore. These troops marched over mountain trails and swooped down on Forts Clinton and Montgomery. Against a determined assault with the bayonet, the Americans held out until dark, then escaped, knowing they were badly outnumbered. The chain and barricade across the river were destroyed, many cannon and their ammunition seized and, when an untoward wind trapped the little patriot flotilla that had anchored off the forts, the ships had to be put to the torch.

Sitting in the cabin of the flagship, Sir Henry dashed off a note to Burgoyne: "*Nous y voici* and nothing now between us but Gates. I sincerely hope this little success may facilitate your operations. . . I heartily wish you success." Fretting in his camp near Freeman's Farm, Burgoyne waited for the message that never came, for the messenger had been captured. If Burgoyne had received it, it would have brought only false hopes. Sir Henry sent a small force upriver to burn Esopus but, on the heels of this minor success, he was handed a message from Howe in Philadelphia asking for reinforcements. So he went back down the Hudson and Burgoyne was left to his own resources.

The situation on the shore of the upper Hudson was changing daily. As the weather turned steadily colder, British rations were cut. Sickness and discontent sapped morale. Deserters crept out of camp in the dark, heading back to Canada and safety. But on the American side, morale was improving.

October 7 saw the second Battle of Saratoga, sometimes called the Battle of Bemis Heights. The battle plan was but little altered. Gates still held the heights and Burgoyne sought to drive him off toward the river with a wide flanking movement. Once again, Fraser led the flanking forces but this time Von Reidesel held the center. In the fortified camp behind the British lines remained a motley group of reserves, wounded men, hostlers, bakers, and the wives of many of the higher officers, including the Baroness Von Reidesel with her three small children. The picnic or promenade that Gentleman Johnny had confidently planned was about to come to a bloody close for both the fighting men and those in the rear who had slowed his marches and cost him many sorely needed rations. Fraser began his sweep and was almost immediately caught in the sights of Daniel Morgan's riflemen. The British were forced back into their redoubts but held firm, as did the German mercenaries nearer the river.

At the same time, General Enoch Poor led a body of eight hundred Americans against the British left flank. In this force were Continentals from New Hampshire, militia from New York, one regiment under Philip Van Cortlandt, and two regiments of Connecticut militia, all of whom had seen considerable service. Despite heavy fire, Poor's brigade turned the British left. Artillery on both sides kept up a heavy cannonading. In the cellar of a stone house near Freeman's Farm, Baroness Von Reidesel sought to protect her children as well as other women in her party, and at the same time to nurse the wounded brought in from the field. Cannonballs pierced the building's walls, but the work of mercy went on.

For a time the Germans held firm in the center with the

help of British regulars retreating from both flanks, but Morgan and Dearborn, with the latter's light infantry, kept up the pressure. General Benedict Arnold, who for days had been feuding with Gates, had been ordered off the field by the latter; but he appeared among the Carolina riflemen and urged them to shoot General Simon Fraser, who had done an outstanding job of rallying British troops. When a bullet knocked Fraser from his horse, the spirit of resistance on that flank collapsed and the tide of battle definitely turned toward the patriots. A little later in the afternoon Arnold led a foolhardy charge straight into the mouths of the British guns in the center. Behind him streamed men from Learned's brigade, and scattered men from Morgan's, Wesson's, and Livingston's regiments. A bullet struck Arnold's thigh, but the attack carried. To all intents and purposes, the conflict was over.

Unfortunately, bitter fighting in the high command at Gate's headquarters clouded the victory. Arnold noisily claimed that he had won the battle for Gates. Others insisted that the English, having been so badly mauled, would have surrendered sooner or later anyway. Burgoyne himself gave credit to Arnold. But even at this late date the controversy occasionally reappears among military historians.

It took ten days for the surrender details to be worked out. Burgoyne sought to gain time, still hoping that Sir Henry would appear behind Gate's lines. Then he wheedled Gates into agreeing that the surrender was a convention, not a capitulation. In the end the British marched away, their arms thrown down, between silent ranks of American soldiers. A small party of Indian warriors and their squaws were given a special guard to save them from angry farmers who had witnessed what these braves had done when they were victorious.

The Hudson River had never been the scene of such a crucial battle before, nor has it seen one like it since. It was a turning point of the war. Not only was a fourth of the British strength in America defeated, but now the patriot forces were convinced that they could fight as well as the best of Europe's regulars. Poor Gentleman Johnny! All his fond dreams had been shattered

BURGOYNE'S SURRENDER AFTER THE BATTLE OF SARATOGA

Following the battle of Saratoga, it took ten days to arrange the terms under which the British General, "Gentleman Johnny" Burgoyne, agreed to surrender to General Horatio Gates. This version of the surrender scene is from Jacques Milbert's *Picturesque Itinerary of the Hudson River,* originally published in 1828–1829.

Sleepy Hollow Restorations

by men he thought could never become soldiers. He had written in one of his letters that his enemy "have no men of military science." Perhaps they had no formal training, to be sure, but they were becoming battle-wise. Philip Van Cortlandt, it is said, had detected the British when they first took a position above Freeman's Farm and saved the Americans from an unexpected attack; Stark had known what to do with the blundering German mercenaries; Kosciuszko had sensed where to build his entrenchments; and Arnold, Morgan, Poor, even Gates, had made the best of every situation on the battlefield.

Saratoga was undoubtedly a turning point. Had Sir Henry Clinton held the Highlands and fortified them, the war might have turned out differently. Washington's lateral communications would have been severed and either New England or the South could have been defeated piecemeal. But Clinton was ordered back to New York City by Howe, now in trouble in Philadelphia.

Overseas the effect of the patriots' victory at Saratoga and the withdrawal of the British from the Highlands was electrifying. In France, King Louis XVI saw in the Saratoga victory a sign that the Americans could stand up to British might. Tension rose between France and England and by the next spring they were at war in name if not in fact. Holland joined the alliance against Britain, and Spain, though reluctant to recognize the new democratic-minded republic across the Atlantic, nonetheless undertook meaningful hostilities against her old enemy, England. It is not too much to claim that much of this took place because the Hudson remained in American hands.

There was jubilation in Albany but deep misgivings in British-occupied New York City. In the city, far removed from the scene of battle, it was hard to believe there was disaster elsewhere. Parties, fancy dress balls, dinners, and visits back and forth between officers on the ships and merchants on shore continued despite the upheaval of the times. The closest fighting was taking place in Westchester and Putnam Counties, where well-to-do New Yorkers, such as Beverly Robinson and Oliver De Lancey had recruited thousands of Loyalists in the region around the city and led them into battle against former neighbors and friends.

The waters of the harbor teemed with British shipping. At least 150 small sloops and cutters were bringing in food from the farms of Staten Island, Long Island, and middle Jersey. Larger vessels came and went with cargoes from the West Indies, and great convoys of merchantmen protected by heavily armed ships of the line transported goods from England. With such power and wealth, how could one-fourth of all the British troops in North America have been overwhelmed? Patriots like William Marriner could have told them: courage and devotion to a lofty cause.

Although no major campaigns occurred in the Hudson Valley for more than a year after Burgoyne's surrender, there was no peace. Day after day, within the Neutral Ground of Westchester and across the river in Bergen County, neighbor fought neighbor. There were countless nasty little ambuscades, night raids, and brief but bloody encounters. Upstream from the scene of these guerrilla activities the Americans were busy making the Highlands into an impregnable stronghold. Clinton's success at Stony Point and the end run by Vaughn leading to the burning of Kingston had made it clear that stronger fortifications were needed. Washington himself ordered the work started, saying that West Point was the "key to America." A French engineer, de La Radière, drew the plans and Samuel Parsons, with his Connecticut brigade, began the construction in January, 1778. This was the best location for blocking the river. The site of the fort on the western bank was high, too high for shells from warships to reach. It rose abruptly from the shore right where the river made a double right-angle turn. This turn forced the square-rigged vessels of that era to lose headway by altering their course, making them easy targets for the guns in the shore batteries above.

Parson's men erected Fort Arnold, later renamed Fort Clinton, on the lip of the plateau and, with the help of General Kosciuszko, installed water batteries and a system of redoubts that made flanking unlikely. On the land side Forts Putnam,

Webb, and Wyllis were built to serve the same purpose. Finally a massive iron chain was stretched across the Hudson to Constitution Island. This chain was a symbol of patriot determination never again to let the English use the Hudson to divide the new nation. For its time, it was an impressive undertaking. Its manufacture, transportation, and emplacement took months. Iron for the links was mined in the hills of northern Jersey and around the lower Catskills. Day after day the furnaces glowed as the ore was transformed into iron bars. Then at the Sterling Iron Works near Sloatsburg blacksmiths labored at forge and anvil making the bars into links two feet long and two and a quarter inches thick. Heavy farm wagons, pulled by oxen, carried the finished links to New Windsor, upriver from West Point. There they were linked together to form the chain, then fastened again to huge logs used as floats. Finally the chain was allowed to drift downstream and then anchored in place, one end at West Point and the other on the shore of Constitution Island. With the batteries at either end, the chain formed a barrier that brought joy to the heart of every patriot. For a young nation with so little experience in warfare, West Point was a massive fortification. The Marquis de Chastellux spoke for many military men when he marveled at the engineering wonder created "by a people who six years before had scarcely ever seen a cannon."

Washington did not rely on iron and stone alone. Determined to hold the Highlands, he ordered Israel Putnam and his Continentals to man the new fort at West Point. Gates and McDougall held firm at Danbury, Connecticut, where supplies were stored in one of the main depots for the American army, and in between were Baron de Kalb at present-day Patterson and Lord Stirling on the ridge behind Lake Mahopac. For the first time, residents of the valley began to feel secure. Behind this barrier stores were growing at the big supply depot at Fishkill, the Legislature was installed at Newburgh, and Albany had recovered from the fright Burgoyne had aroused the year before. In New York City, Sir Henry Clinton felt the jaws of the patriot vise growing tighter and, as winter came on, he spent a good deal of time planning to strike back when the weather

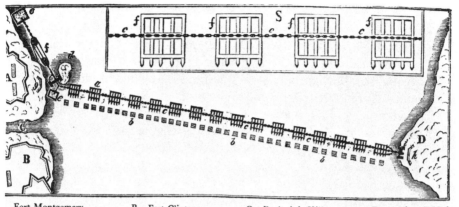

Fort Montgomery.   B   Fort Clinton.   C   Poplopin's Kill.   D   Anthony's Nofe.
   a Floats to Chain.   *b b b* Booms in front of Chain.   *c c c* Chain.
d Rock at which the Chain was fecured with large Iron Roller.   *e e* Cribs and Anchors.
  f Blocks and Purchafe for tightening Chain.   *g h* Ground Batteries for defence of Chain.
      S Section fhowing Floats and Chain.   *c c c* Chain.   *f f f* Floats.

The New-York Historical Society

CHAIN ACROSS THE HUDSON AT WEST POINT

The chain across the Hudson at West Point, designed to prevent
British ships from sailing up the river, was an important part of
the American defenses. This engraving is said to have been
"copied from the original Map of the Position of the Chain,
found among the papers of the Secret Committee" which
intended to betray the fortification to the enemy.

turned fair. His plan was actually born in London, where Britain's leaders had decided that the Hudson was the key to the war in America. With the river in their hands, they argued, they could handle the rebellion in stages and thus with Tory help restore control.

Late in May 1778, Clinton embarked his troops at King's Bridge and moved up the Hudson. He had six thousand men, the best of his army, including British regulars, Tory regiments, Hessians, and a small contingent of dragoons. Seventy sailing vessels and fifty flat-bottomed barges moved menacingly through the lower river, across the Tappan Zee and then to the vicinity of King's Ferry, twelve miles below West Point. Guarding the chief lateral communications link between New England and the other states were two weak forts, Stony Point on the west shore and Verplanck's Point or Fort Lafayette on the east. Feinting toward the latter fortification, Clinton led his troops ashore in a fog and came up on the inland side of Stony Point, capturing the forty men there without firing a shot. The next morning he bombarded Fort Lafayette and, when more troops went ashore on the east bank, the defenders fled. Clinton hoped that Washington might react to this incursion near the Highlands but the American commander in chief had other plans for retaliating. He called in General Anthony Wayne and asked him if he thought he could recapture Stony Point. "I'll storm Hell if you'll only plan it," the fiery Wayne is reported to have said.

The two generals discussed the problem for weeks as Clinton carefully transformed the captured stronghold into a virtually impregnable position. The topography was in the British general's favor. At high tide the fort was actually an island separated from the mainland by a flooded marsh. Across this low land a single causeway gave access to the fort. On the crest of the hill, he had his engineers build two rows of abatis—sharpened tree branches facing the enemy and interlaced with timber palisades.

A month and a half after the two forts had been captured "Mad Anthony" Wayne mustered his force of thirteen hundred men—veterans from Connecticut, Massachusetts, Virginia, Pennsylvania, and North Carolina—at a rendezvous thirteen

WEST POINT WITH ITS FORTIFICATIONS, 1780

During the Revolutionary War, West Point would have appeared as it does in this early rendering, "West-Point, with its Fortifications &c in 1780," drawn and engraved by J. Smillie "from the original drawing made in 1780 by L'Enfant, Engineer, U.S. Army."

Sleepy Hollow Restorations

miles from Stony Point. The next afternoon they started marching south, around the shoulder of Dunderberg Mountain, along farm roads and wooded paths. No one was there to see them and hurry off to report the news, for all the residents had been sent away days before. No dog barked in betrayal; they had all been killed by scouts. By evening the attackers were at the edge of the marsh, their guns emptied of powder but bayonets in place. With squads racing ahead with axes to clear paths through the abatis, Wayne moved his men forward in silence, each step through the waist-high water taken with infinite care to avoid an alarm. Wayne promised the first man inside the enemy position a $500 prize and smaller prizes for the next four. Like angry wolverines the troops tore at the abatis where the axmen had chopped narrow paths. Shouting "The fort's our own!", they dashed up the slope and into the redoubts, bayonets flashing in the light of campfires. The defenders were good men; a battalion of the 17th (Leicestershire) Foot, a grenadier company of Fraser's 71st Highlanders, a detachment of the Royal (Tory) Americans, and the gunners at the batteries. For thirty minutes they fought hand to hand, but the surprise was too great. Wayne lost fifteen men killed and eighty wounded. The British lost 63 killed, 70 wounded, and 543 captured.

Up and down the Hudson went word of Mad Anthony's great victory. The Americans had won with cold steel against the best the enemy had to offer. A French lieutenant colonel, Francois de Fleury, won the $500 prize but a grateful Congress gave every man a share of the prize money for the captured supplies and ammunition. The victory at Stony Point had scant strategic value inasmuch as the fortification had to be abandoned in the face of British power at the mouth of the river, but as a morale factor it gave the Americans a decided lift and seriously discouraged the British.

There was one more major battle on the Hudson before the valley quieted down for more than a year. It grew out of Washington's desire for another limited operation to keep Clinton off balance. Some historians say that it actually originated in the desire of Major Henry ("Light Horse Harry") Lee to win the

GENERAL ANTHONY WAYNE

The fiery leader was known in his day as "Mad Anthony" Wayne
because of his willingness to undertake even the most dangerous
assignments. This illustration is reproduced from one of the steel
engravings in the volume of *Illustrations to Irving's Life of
Washington*, published in New York in 1859.

sort of glory Mad Anthony Wayne had achieved. In his *Life of Washington*, Washington Irving stated that "Stony Point had piqued his [Lee's] emulation." Whatever the reason, Lee learned through spies and patriot farmers that the British fortifications at Paulus Hook on the Jersey shore across from lower Manhattan were undermanned. He proposed an assault and Washington authorized a hit-and-run attack. With the help of the glamorous Captain Allan McLane, one of Washington's ablest scouts, Lee planned for a night attack. On the morning of August 18, with four hundred men he marched out of his camp at Paramus with eighteen miles of slogging ahead of them. As they approached what is now Jersey City there was a dispute over seniority and many Virginians left the force. Lee went on, hours late, and began his assault just before dawn of the nineteenth instead of at midnight. Paulus Hook, like Stony Point, was separated from the mainland by sandy spits, salt marshes, and tidal swamps. The Americans waded through the morass breast-deep, with axmen in the van to clear away a path through the abatis. British sentinels heard the noise and opened fire but the Americans charged ahead, attacking various redoubts and a central citadel built of heavy logs. Their impetus carried them to a quick victory, although the British commander, Major William Sutherland, took refuge inside the strongest redoubt with about fifty Hessians and refused to surrender.

Reaction came swiftly from the British in Manhattan. Guns were readied as men put out in small boats from the island and from men-of-war anchored in the river. Remembering Washington's orders for a quick assault and as quick a retreat, Lee withdrew. The retreat was a neck-and-neck race with Tory forces on horseback posing a threat all the way. At the Hackensack, where boats were supposed to be waiting to ferry the men to safety, Lee found no one. His men had waited but, when time dragged on considerably past the assembly hour, they had gone off, leaving the party stranded. Fighting a rearguard action most of the way, the Americans were exhausted from the long march, the night assault, and the tense wait in the marshes. They finally dragged themselves into Paramus with 158 prisoners, marking another hour of glory for the cause of independence.

All through this period of strife on the Hudson marked by the capture of Stony Point and Paulus Hook, Major General Benedict Arnold, hero of Valcour Island, victorious at Saratoga and one of the ablest of Washington's field officers, was negotiating with the British to turn traitor. Luck played into the enemy's hands when Washington appointed Arnold to command West Point. Letters went back and forth between Arnold and Sir Henry Clinton, one bearing Arnold's demand that he receive twenty thousand pounds if he succeeded in handing over the Point to the British. In another note he insisted that final arrangements be conducted in person between himself and an officer close to the British high command. Slyly Arnold proceeded to weaken the American defenses. He reduced the force at the Point by sending two hundred men to cut wood near Fishkill and let the chain across the Hudson fall into disrepair. Instead of moving into the quarters provided at the fort, Arnold went to live in the home of Colonel Beverly Robinson, the wealthy Tory who led a spy service for the British and had moved to the city for his own safety.

This was the situation when residents of the lower Hudson saw His Majesty's man-of-war *Vulture* sail lazily upstream and then anchor off Teller's Point. Late on the night of September 21, a boat appeared from the shadows, rowed out to the *Vulture*, and returned to the west bank with a passenger. That passenger was Major John André, aide-de-camp to General Clinton. For almost four hours Arnold and André discussed the betrayal of West Point at a rendezvous near a house owned by William Smith, Royal Chief Justice of New York, and occupied by his brother Joshua. It was here that coincidence brought good fortune to the American patriots. André was supposed to go back aboard the *Vulture* and so make his way to the city, but Colonel James Livingston, leader of militia forces in the area, thwarted this scheme. Livingston had moved two heavy pieces of artillery into place on Teller's Point, planning to punish the *Vulture* for considering the Hudson her safe, unchallenged thoroughfare.

As Arnold gazed, horrified, from a window in the Smith

house, the guns on the east bank began to find the range and pummeled the *Vulture* badly. Riddled with grape and suffering from holes below the waterline caused by solid shot, the British sloop raised anchor and managed to escape downstream. Major André was left inside the American lines, the plans to West Point and other incriminating documents hidden in his boot. Joshua Smith rowed him across the Hudson and went with him as far as Pine's Bridge, where he left the young English officer on his own. André had a pass issued by Arnold several days before, informing American officers on the line above the Neutral Ground that a "John Anderson" might enter the lines from New York and be sent on with impunity to Arnold's headquarters. Hoping this would suffice, André reined his mount toward Pleasantville, to try to reach White Plains and safety by that route. When he learned that American patrols were in the area, he turned west to the Hudson, reaching the river near Tarrytown. At the bridge just outside the little village three armed men barred his way.

Here the true facts in the case are shrouded in obscurity. Some contend that the three men, John Paulding, Isaac Van Wart, and David Williams, were homespun heroes, eager to win the war. Others, basing their conclusions on later information, have maintained that the three were nothing more than freebooters, out for any loot they could take. At any rate, they searched André, found the damning plans in his boot, and took him prisoner to Lieutenant Colonel John Jameson, in command at North Castle. André's pass was of no help to him now. Jameson, wondering how a "Mr. Anderson" who was supposed to come up from the city was actually apprehended riding from the opposite direction, sent a courier with word of the arrest to General Arnold at the Robinson house.

Arnold and his aides were breakfasting, awaiting the arrival of Washington from the military supply depot at Danbury. Peggy, his wife, was primping in the boudoir upstairs when the messenger dismounted at the door. The traitor read the message about his accomplice's seizure, excused himself, and tore upstairs to tell Peggy, who had been a party to the treachery all along. Then rushing outdoors again, Arnold told his aides that he had an hour's special duty to perform at West Point and to inform Washington that he would soon return. Instead, the traitor jumped into his barge and ordered his servants to row him downstream to where he boarded the damaged *Vulture*, still making emergency repairs and licking her wounds from Livingston's guns. André lived but a few days before he was hanged as a spy at Tappan, within sight of the home of Johannes DeWint where Washington was staying.

Legend has it that Washington ordered the shutters of the DeWint house closed on the day of the hanging. Both Englishmen and Americans mourned André's death, as they had Nathan Hale's. Many regretted that the neck in the hempen noose was not that of the traitor Benedict Arnold.

The large-scale campaigns and fierce battles between trained men shifted from the Hudson. Washington remained in the north, sometimes at Newburgh or New Windsor, sometimes at posts in New Jersey. Most of the troops he did not need to keep Clinton pinned down in New York City were sent south where Nathanael Greene, Daniel Morgan, Lafayette, and others were fighting Cornwallis. But he bore in mind the possibility that he might still force Clinton out of the city at the mouth of the Hudson. Once Washington organized an attack against the British posts around Spuyten Duyvil, but the enemy was too strongly entrenched. Having no siege guns, he abandoned the plan. Instead, he journeyed to Wethersfield in Connecticut to confer with General Rochambeau, leader of the French expeditionary force in Rhode Island. Rochambeau got along famously with the American commander in chief. The two men quickly agreed on another plan, made more appealing by word from de Grasse at sea that he would soon be off the Chesapeake capes with his huge fleet. With Cornwallis retreating into tidewater Virginia, here was a chance to strike a heavy blow for independence. So they decided to move swiftly from the Hudson to Virginia.

Leaving Heath with half of the American force in the Highlands, Washington took the balance of his army and all of the French troops across the Hudson at King's Ferry. The French

MAJOR JOHN ANDRÉ

Inset below this aquatint portrait of Major John André is a reproduction of his self-portrait, said to have been sketched on the morning of the day fixed for his execution as a spy (October 2, 1780). The portrait itself has been identified only as being by an artist named Edwards.

had already marched clear across Rhode Island and Connecticut but were in fine spirits. It took four full days for the troops to be ferried across the river, ample time for Loyalist spies to give Clinton detailed information about the movement. But Clinton was a stubborn, unimaginative man. He could not conceive of the enemy marching overland all the way to Virginia; so when Washington sent a light force as if to attack Staten Island, the British commander relaxed. Not until the troops reached Philadelphia did Clinton realize that the war was shifting inexorably to the southern theater.

The story of Yorktown belongs elsewhere, but many a man raised on the Hudson found glory in the climactic battle of the revolution. Philip Van Cortlandt was there with the 2nd New York Regiment; Alexander Hamilton's battalion was there, and so was Lamb's New York artillery. So too was Van Schaick's 1st New York. When the attack against Cornwallis began, there must have been a thousand men from New York in the ranks, probably more than half of them from the Hudson Valley. Victory was sweet, but the suffering was far from over. Washington sent the bulk of his New York, Delaware, and Maryland regulars south to reinforce Greene and led the balance of his men back to the Hudson Highlands, to keep a watchful eye on Clinton. The latter, moving with that exasperating slowness that so annoyed his chiefs back in London, had embarked with seven thousand troops on the very day Cornwallis surrendered. Finding that he was too late, he sailed back into New York harbor.

As extended efforts were made to draft a treaty, there was still no peace in the northern environs of New York City. Skinners and Cowboys—predatory bands who roamed over the Neutral Ground—robbed and pillaged even as they professed allegiance to the two causes, and in many isolated rural districts looting was a way of life. While John Jay of Bedford was in Paris, negotiating for an honorable peace, his home county of Westchester was seared by the internecine fighting, as another year passed and the talks still dragged on.

Late in November, Washington quit Newburgh to make his way into New York City, which the British were evacuating.

GEORGE WASHINGTON RIDES TRIUMPHANT INTO NEW YORK CITY

The colored lithograph on page 91 depicts the triumphal entry of General George Washington into New York City after the evacuation of the British, November 25, 1783.

WASHINGTON TAKING LEAVE OF HIS OFFICERS

George Washington's farewell to his officers at Fraunces Tavern in lower Manhattan, December 4, 1783; lithograph after a painting by Harry A. Ogden (1856–1936).

Most of his staff were from other states, so it is only fitting that a resident of the Hudson Valley be allowed to describe the last ride down the river. Pierre Van Cortlandt, the lieutenant governor, whose home had been ravaged by the guerrillas and whose mills had ground out flour for the hungry American army, narrated it in these words:

> I went from Peekskill Tuesday, the 18th of Nov., in company with his excellency Governor Clinton, Colonel Benson and Colonel Campbell. Lodged that night with General Van Cortlandt [his son Philip] at Croton River, proceeded and lodged Wednesday night at Edward Cowenhovens, where we met General Washington and his aides. The next night lodged with Mr. Frederick Van Cortlandt at Yonkers, after having dined with General Lewis Morris; Friday morning in company with the Commander-in-Chief, as far as the widow Day's at Harlem, where we held a council. Saturday I rode down to Mr. Stuyvesant's; stayed there until Tuesday. *Then Rode Triumphant into the City with the Commander-in-Chief.*

On December 4, Washington took leave of his officers at Fraunces Tavern in lower Manhattan. He was rowed in his barge across the river to the Jersey shore, to go home to the Potomac, leaving the Hudson behind him.

Chapter V

From Sloop to Steamer

Out of the camps along the river marched the weary soldiers, heading for home and families, or starting west for the Ohio country to obtain the hundred acres of free land promised by Congress to each fighting man. The chain across the Hudson was winched up for the last time and the little boatyards like the one at Poughkeepsie run by Van Zandt, Lawrence & Tudor turned from building cutters and schooners to laying down sloops. Now that peace had finally come to the Hudson, there would be great need for sloops.

If there was joy upriver it was muted by sadness whenever Tory families, certain that life was impossible for them under American rule, set out on the long road to new homes. Some piled wagons high with whatever goods they could collect and trudged north along Burgoyne's route, past Lake George, Lake Champlain, and down the Richelieu River until they reached Montreal. Most, however, loaded possessions into sloops and sailed downriver, there to embark in ships made available by the English for the long voyage to Nova Scotia and New Brunswick. More than twenty-eight thousand Tories sailed out of New York harbor for the Canadian Maritime Provinces in 1783, the year the peace treaty was signed. A large share of them had known no other home than the Hudson Valley.

Behind them they left a people eager to get on with the business of peace. While the politicians argued about the best possible government for the country, it seemed almost everyone was going up the Hudson or down, traveling on hundreds of sloops that crowded the narrow reaches in good weather until they resembled flocks of white herons skimming over the water. Food, cattle, and lumber went down the river to New York. Manufactured English goods, hardware, boots and shoes, textiles and kitchenware moved in the other direction.

Something resembling the sloop had been in existence long before the *Half Moon* made her way up the Great River of the Mountains. The Portuguese had a similar craft called a *chalupa*, as did other countries bordering the Mediterranean. The Dutch called it a *sloep* and found it useful on rivers and canals and for duty in the North Sea. Usually a sloop had a single mast with a mainsail, a jib, and, quite often, a topsail. When the Dutch first introduced these craft in the New World they had lee boards, but the center board or keel proved more satisfactory. Whatever their rigging, they were all steered with a long tiller. For inland water service, most were built from sixty-five to seventy-five feet in length and could carry approximately a hundred tons. They were broad of beam, heavy of planking, and often had a rather high quarter-deck; yet, because the mast was stepped far forward, there was ample deck space for cargo or, in passenger service, for sunning and dancing. Carl Carmer described them as built like the Dutchmen's wives, "well rounded in the bow and high aft."

Travel and shipping relied on the sloop because the roads along the river were an ordeal for vehicles; hard and bumpy when the earth was frozen, covered with axledeep mud in the spring and after a rain. Merchants and other large users owned or chartered sloops for their products, but the riding public and the occasional shipper relied on sloops called packets, with room for anyone having the fare. Many of the letters Hudson Valley residents wrote to relatives in the years between the Revolution and the Civil War bore such words of address as "To the care of Capt. A. Weeks with a Pot & Basket," "Care of A. Davids, Sloop *Caroline*, with a basket," or "Care of Capt. T. Brett, Sloop *Levant* with a trunk." These sloop skippers were the freight carriers

96

HUDSON RIVER SLOOP

In the eighteenth and early nineteenth centuries, before the advent of the steamboat, Hudson River sloops carried all sorts of cargo up and down the river. An artist's rendering shows such a sloop being loaded at the wharf of the gristmill at Philipsburg Manor, Upper Mills.

of the early nineteenth century. They were also guardians of single women and small children, deposited in their care, along with all the pots, baskets, and trunks.

It was their obligation to sail safely the one-hundred and fifty miles from New York to Albany with as little delay as possible. They knew full well that "a ship at anchor earns no money for the owner." Good sailors sought to ride the flood tide upriver as far as possible, with foreknowledge of the eccentricities that marked every mile of the stream. Early mariners counted distance on the Hudson by "reaches," many of which bore names. The first stretched along the Palisades, the second into the Tappan Zee, and the third took its name from Haverstraw Bay. Then, in order, came Seylmaker's, Hoge's, Vorsen's, which included the tricky passage through the Highlands, Fisher's, reaching to Esopus, Claverack, Playsier, Vast, and Hunter's.

Tillermen had to think about the winds that slanted off the Palisades, the deep tide that could slow a boat down even when the surface tide was setting in the opposite direction, the way a current passed through a narrow channel hugging one shore; and always they had to be ready to lower sail if a sudden squall blew up. At the gateway to the Highlands under Thunder Mountain sloops would often bounce and roll, stealing the wind from one another, until tide and wind turned to their satisfaction.

If there were such a thing as an ideal voyage, it would approximate this: A sloop would round the Battery at New York on the lip of a flood tide at, say, 6 A.M., reach Newburgh by noon and Poughkeepsie by 2 P.M. Then Hudson would come abeam at 8 or 9 P.M. and, if the wind did not die in the upper reaches, the sloop would tie up at the Albany dock in the early hours as the sun rose over the Berkshires. This twenty-four-hour run was ideal, but seldom attained. On many a trip the winds died at the wrong time, and a small boat had to be put over with oarsmen to keep it from drifting on the rocks; or the wind would come slithering down off the Catskills at such a clip the skipper could do nothing but drop anchor. Often he had to take in canvas on the Tappan Zee when the fog hung so thickly about him he could not see the end of the tiller from the taffrail. It was on nights like this that some of the old Dutch skippers swore they saw Rambout Van Dam rowing his boat downstream, still hoping for a landfall at Spuyten Duyvil.

The tillerman had to have at least one extra sense to tell when he was nearing a ferry crossing, the shoals and sand spits of the upper Hudson, and the rocky points that jutted out from shore in so many places. Some of this extrasensory perception may have been nothing but experience and training handed down from one generation to another. Ferries, of course, were not a new phenomenon. Jeremiah Dobbs, a Swede who settled on the Philipse patent, opened a ferry service that gave the town its name. Then there was Sneden's Landing where Mollie Sneden operated a ferry at the lower end of the Zee.

Year in and year out it took longer to go downstream than it did upstream; but no matter in which direction a sloop sailed the likelihood was that it would take four to seven days rather than the twenty-four hours every skipper aimed at. When the winds were absolutely wrong boats would anchor for a full day or two, giving the passengers a chance to explore the countryside. Travel by sloop was still better than any other mode in the years before steam, and residents of Litchfield County, Connecticut, and the lower Berkshires in Massachusetts would take the stagecoach from Litchfield, Great Barrington, and Lenox, ride across the Dutchess Turnpike to Poughkeepsie, and then take a sloop to New York.

Business was so brisk that captains seldom worried about return cargo. If they unloaded at Albany without prior arrangements they could always take on lumber for New York and Long Island ports for local construction purposes or for shipment across the seas. There was lime, cement, brick, flagstones destined for the city, and cordwood for the iron furnaces. For every passenger packet there were a dozen freight boats that carried people between the small towns. These latter craft were no scented gardens of delight. The forecastle was set apart for cooking over an open hearth built on a brick base to prevent fires. If coal was burned the odor was nauseating, and if wood the sparks were dangerous, often starting small fires in the canvas.

In the early years, sloops were used for sturgeon fishing full-time or whenever there was a lull in the freight and passenger business. These fish, running to 250 pounds in weight, leaped and frolicked like children at play, sometimes falling stunned and helpless on the deck, and saving the fishermen the trouble of catching them. Known locally as "Albany beef," the fish commanded good prices in the port city. From the first day the white man had sailed the Hudson, he had marveled at the sturgeon and counted heavily on it as a source of food. In the beginning he fished the way the Indians did, at night, with pine knots burning at the ends of poles to attract the fish. The Indians harpooned them with spears, and it was a long time before the white man turned to faster methods. Often passengers on sloops caught by adverse weather watched as fishermen rowed out from the little villages along the bank to catch sturgeon, using the same old Indian technique. Some even tried it themselves to while away the evening hours.

This was just one of the things that made a cruise on the Hudson a pleasant adventure. The scenery changed with the hour and the winds and, as there were no noises of engines or motors, travelers could hear quail piping in the fields flanking the stream and often catch the rumbling thunder of ruffed grouse fleeing some enemy in the forest. Washington Irving was not exaggerating when he had one of his characters say that a trip up the Hudson was as exciting as a trip to Europe. This description from the early Dutch days was accurate right up until the advent of the steamboat:

> The sloops were often many days on the way; the cautious navigator taking in sail when it blew fresh, and coming to anchor at night, and stopping to send the boat ashore for milk or tea, without which it was impossible for the worthy old lady passengers to subsist, and there were the much talked of perils of the Tappan Zee, and the Highlands. In short, a prudent Dutch burgher would talk of such a voyage

HUDSON HIGHLANDS

Sailing vessels of all sorts would have dotted the Hudson during the years before the advent of steamboats. A typical scene is represented in this print by W. H. Bartlett (1809–1854).

Sleepy Hollow Restorations

for months, and even years, beforehand; and never undertook it without putting his affairs in order, making his will, and having prayers said for him in the Low Dutch Churches.

Ninety percent of the sloops that sailed the Hudson were of the one-hundred-ton size but, as business boomed in the west and more cargoes came to New York for transshipment inland, the yards began turning out larger craft. The *Utica* was the largest, built in Albany to haul 220 tons at a time. From the end of the War of Independence until the middle of the nineteenth century, there were boatyards at Albany, Hudson, Coxsackie, Newburgh, Poughkeepsie, Rondout, Fishkill, Cornwall, and a dozen other places.

The passenger packets and heavy-duty freight boats alike bore beautiful names. There were the *General Washington* and *General Putnam*, the *American Eagle* and *Green County Tanner*, the *General Van Cortlandt* and the *Twilight*, *Winder*, *Victory*, and *Star*. They carried ladies in fancy dresses and elegant bonnets to the races at Saratoga, drummers with housewares bound for the Mohawk Valley towns, loggers, tanners, stonecutters, and mule drivers. They caught fire and burned to the water's edge, broke up when caught in the ice, sank in sudden blows that coursed down the Race near Anthony's Nose, and ran aground in the flats of the upper river and rotted away. They raced the first steamboats and held their own for years; one of them, the *W. W. Reynolds*, beating downriver off Blue Point near Poughkeepsie, rammed her bowsprit into the boiler of the steamer *Francis Skiddy* and caused the death of firemen and passengers. For two hundred years they plied the Hudson, making history as well as watching it. When Alexander Hamilton rowed across to Weehawken on the morning of July 11, 1804, to meet Aaron Burr on the field of honor, his oared boat threaded its way through sloops dotting the lower reaches of the river. When his mortally wounded body was taken back across the stream to a friend's house in Greenwich Village, the boat was observed by skippers on other sloops.

From Sloop to Steamer

Sloops had carried men and material for the fortification of West Point and helped supply the station when it was the base for the "Corps of Artillerists and Engineers" after the war. On July 4, 1802, when ten cadets entered as the first class at the U. S. Military Academy at the Point, sloop skippers saluted them from the river below. Built by hand out of stout white oak and locust, manned by crews from scores of river towns, they served the people well and helped a young nation grow.

I left New York on Monday at four o'clock and arrived at Clermont, the seat of Chancellor Livingston, at one o'clock on Tuesday, time, twenty-four hours, distance, one hundred and ten miles. On Wednesday I departed from the Chancellor's at nine o'clock in the morning and arrived at Albany at five in the afternoon; distance, forty miles, time, eight hours. The sum is one hundred and fifty miles in thirty-two hours, equal to near five miles an hour.

These simple, almost casual, words, written in the dry-as-dust manner of a timetable or a sheriff's land sale notice, told the world that the age of sail was dead. Steam had conquered distance and time.

The man who wrote them was Robert Fulton and, although he was delighted to give the lie to thousands of skeptics and doubting Thomases, it was not out of malice or meanness. Other accounts of the day, August 17, 1807, on which the steamship *Clermont* went from New York to Albany with no propulsive power save steam, were considerably more exciting than the inventor's own words.

One farmer, watching the steamboat move up the stream against current and wind, said it was "a sawmill on a raft spitting fire," and a sailor described it as "a monster moving on the waters defying wind and tide, breathing flames and smoke, and lighting its path by the fires which it vomited." From the time of the ancient Phoenicians and even before, vessels of one sort or another had been propelled on the water by the wind or by men

103

THE *Clermont* AS DRAWN BY ROBERT FULTON

The inventor Robert Fulton (1765–1815) produced this wash
drawing of the steamship *Clermont* as originally designed.

at the oars. Now all this was past. "Fulton's Folly" had proved itself: it was a commercial success, and a tool that would revolutionize the world.

Robert Fulton was a Pennsylvania boy of Scottish ancestry who liked to tinker with things mechanical. It is unclear how much he knew of other attempts to harness the steam engine—then in its infancy—to the propulsion of boats. James Rumsey, with General Washington looking on, had tried to use a jet of water driven by pumps as a power source. It was a failure. John Fitch, John Stevens, and Elijah Ormsbee all had tried and failed, although Stevens did succeed in getting from Hoboken to Manhattan in his boat. After the Revolutionary War, Fulton went to Paris and worked to devise a torpedo. Then he developed a steamboat which, however, sank at its pier on the Seine because the engine was too heavy for the wooden vessel.

About this time, Robert Livingston, another man of Scottish ancestry and owner of one of the largest estates on the Hudson, was appointed United States Ambassador to France. When the two came together in Paris, they quickly agreed to collaborate on perfecting the steamboat. Livingston had the money, prestige, and influence. Fulton, for his part, had the inventive genius and the patience.

After ordering a steam engine built to his specifications in England, Fulton shifted operations from Paris to New York, and had the boat itself, the *Clermont*, constructed on the East River. She was 130 feet long, had a 16-foot beam, drew 28 inches of water, and had open paddle wheels on each side. She was rated at 160 tons and her one cylinder was 24 inches in diameter with a 4-foot stroke.

That August afternoon in 1807 bore many of the aspects of a carnival. Thousands lined the shore as the official party went on board. Fulton ordered the engine engaged and the craft moved out into the stream a few hundred feet. Then it stopped, drifting ignominiously as spectators on shore jeered and yelled "I told you so!" Fulton, unworried, addressed the crowd: "If you indulge me a half hour I will either go on or abandon the voyage." Going below, he made a slight adjustment, the wheels started

ROBERT FULTON

Self-portrait inscribed "To Henry Eckford with my friendship this portrait of myself." Eckford was a well-known shipbuilder who constructed the steamship *Robert Fulton.*

churning, and the *Clermont* moved off, with everyone on shore either wildly cheering or struck dumb in amazement.

It was reported that some captains of sloops dived below in terror when they saw the *Clermont* steam past. Others tried to race the steamboat but soon gave up the unequal contest. The trip upriver was an event to remember. On board were Chancellor Robert Livingston and members of his family as well as various political leaders. On the shore at each village and landing, incredulous people gathered to shout, wave, and clap hands, and blow the whistles of foundries and manufacturing plants. Fulton and his cronies sang old Scottish ballads, the refrains echoing from the cliffs of Storm King, Dunderberg, and Anthony's Nose. There were pretty women on board, too, one of them Livingston's cousin, Harriet, who spent as much time gazing at the inventor as she did at the sights along the shore. Later that evening the reason for the ardent looks was made known. After the party had dined well at the Livingston manor house, the Chancellor announced that Fulton and Harriet were betrothed. More bottles were brought up from the cellar, and the guests did not retire until long after midnight.

From one end of the young country to the other, news of Fulton's steamboat was received with a mixture of disbelief and glowing pride. Once people accepted the fact that the event had actually taken place they shared in the reflected glory. The young nation had now shown the world it was no backwoods country of farmers and hunters, as the English had long been insisting. Hudson River folk, except for a few discomfited sloop captains, were proudest of all. Several attempts were made deliberately to damage the *Clermont*, but the state legislature passed a law making such attempts public offenses and setting stiff fines and prison terms for them.

Fulton and Livingston now advertised for passengers and cargo, boasting that weather would not delay their packet. They persuaded the legislature to expand their monopoly to all steam travel in the state and the *Clermont* kept operating during the year until the Hudson became so clogged with ice that Fulton thought it much too dangerous to continue. During the winter the *Clermont* was enlarged and renamed the *North River*.

To all those who had suffered the aches and pains of stagecoach travel on the bumpy Albany Post Road, to those who had complained of fog and adverse winds that kept sloops tied up or anchored in midstream, the steamboat was a magnificent substitute. What did it matter that many had to sleep communal style with from twelve to twenty-four companions in a couple of large cabins? They were happy their womenfolk had a cabin to themselves, and men removed their boots in obedience to a sign that said the penalty for noncompliance would be $1.50 and 50 cents each half-hour thereafter if they kept them on. Anyone who smoked in one of the inside cabins was fined and the money spent to buy wine for the others. Fulton and Livingston wanted no damage done to their vessel, even expressly forbidding anyone from sitting on the dining-room table.

Travel by steamboat in the early 1800s was by no means inexpensive. There was a minimum of $1 for any trip under twenty miles. Other charges were $2 to Verplanck's Point, $2.50 to West Point, $3 to Newburgh, $5 to Hudson, and $7 to Albany, from New York City. Affluent passengers used the Fulton-Livingston Line almost exclusively, forgetting the peace and beauty of travel by sloop. The captain's lists for the *North River* read like a page from a Social Register of long ago:

> H. W. Livingston, Lady & Daughter
> Mr. P. V. Rensalaer & Lady
> Mr. [John] Jay
> Captain Bogert & Daughter
> Gov. Lewis & Lady & blk. girl
> Mr. Cuyler, Lady·& Ser't
> Miss Duane & Miss Van Kleeck
> Nicholas Roosevelt
> Mr. Peter Schuyler

The passenger list for 1808 also mentions a Mrs. Yates who brought with her 471 pounds of baggage up the Hudson! Two years after the *Clermont* made world history, Fulton

STEAMBOAT *Clermont* OR *North River*

Robert Fulton's steamboat *Clermont*, enlarged and renamed the *North River*, was painted in 1861 in watercolor on paper by Richard Varick DeWitt.

had another steamboat, the *Car of Neptune*, in service and soon thereafter she was joined by the *Paragon* and the *Firefly*. They were larger craft, but the engines took up so much space that there was little room left for cargo. Traffic continued at a brisk rate, even after Fulton and Livingston died, but the monopoly had angered others who were anxious to get their boats on the Hudson. The weak link in the law granting the monopoly was a clause that would have extended it to the shore of New Jersey, a state very proud of its own rights. Eventually lawsuits were initiated and one, Gibbons *v*. Ogden, in which Daniel Webster represented the plaintiffs, reached all the way to the Supreme Court. Webster argued that the people of New York should be protected from the monopoly, and Chief Justice John Marshall ruled that the New York statute was "repugnant to the Constitution and laws of the United States."

Within a decade the Hudson was alive with steamboats flying the flags of a score of companies. From then on the procession of boats not only grew longer but more splendid and ornate. Isaac Newton of Hudson built, traded, and bought steamboats until he owned more than a hundred passenger craft, barges, and freight boats. He called his company the People's Line, and men like Daniel Drew, Erastus Corning, and Dean Richmond invested in the company's stock, knowing that this often brought at least temporary fame because boats were named for the individual capitalists.

It was an era of plush opulence, of well-padded chairs and "sophas" and well-padded ladies and gentlemen. An Englishman, having traveled to Albany on one of the steamboats, marveled that women were given the best quarters, and

No man is admitted into the dining saloon until all the ladies are seated at the table, when they rush in pellmell. After that should a lady require either, the chair is, without ceremony, taken from under you and the plate from before you.

Steam power attracted many promoters, none more colorful

THE MARY POWELL PASSING THE GATE OF THE HIGHLANDS.

The New-York Historical Society

STEAMBOAT *Mary Powell* PASSING THE GATE OF THE HIGHLANDS

"Within a decade the Hudson was alive with steamboats flying the flags of a score of companies." This engraving of the steamboat *Mary Powell* is taken from an Ulster County (New York) Atlas from the year 1875.

than the skipper of a small sail ferryboat that ran between Staten Island and Manhattan. His name was Cornelius Vanderbilt and he learned early how to fight for business with no holds barred. He bought a steamboat, advertised that his line would carry people to Albany for lower rates than any other, and promised bigger, faster, fancier boats in the future. During those years the Manhattan and Albany waterfronts took on the aspect of a turbulent carnival. Each line hired leather-lunged "runners" to drum up trade, and these pitchmen, strong of arm and weak on justice, did everything but kidnap passengers. Anyone appearing on the streets near the piers with a carpetbag or bundle was fair prey. The runners lied to timid old ladies about the safety of the boats, divided families between rival boats, and threatened one another with knives and broken bottles. The rivalry intensified until owners started cutting rates in hope of capturing passengers. Fares dropped from $7 and $10 to a dollar, then to ten cents. Indeed, one line temporarily did away with all fares, owners reclaiming their investment by charging travelers exorbitant prices for food and drinks.

All through this period of wild competition the people along the Hudson took pride in the fact that no river on earth carried so much traffic powered by steam. In 1840, there were a hundred floating palaces on the Hudson and ten years later this number had jumped to one hundred and fifty. More than a million passengers were counted on the river in 1851.

Robert Fulton had exulted in making the trip to Albany in thirty-two hours. Before he died in 1815 this record was beaten many times and by the 1830s the trip had been whittled down to ten hours. During the Civil War the *Chauncey Vibbard* cut the time to seven hours, making the entire trip in daylight.

Small boys, playing at the river's edge, knew the steamboats as familiarly as they knew their brothers and sisters. They could recognize them by their foghorns, by their silhouettes, even by the way they were steered when passing other boats or rounding dangerous points. They knew the house flags that flew above the pilot houses identifying such lines as the Troy Line, the O & D Line, the Steam Navigation Company, the North

River Association Line, the Union Line, even one called the Connecticut Line. Many of these lads dreamed of being riverboat captains, envying the bearded men who paced behind the glass windows of the pilot houses, resplendent in brass-buttoned, gold-braided uniforms. As the number of boats and passengers mounted, many of them saw their dreams come true.

Fulton's own first, full-time skipper was Captain Samuel Jenkins, who had the wheel on the *North River*. Life on the Hudson must have agreed with most of the early masters, for they lived to a ripe old age. Captain R. G. Cruttenden of the first *Constellation* boasted he had made 1,162 trips on her without damage to a single one of the 172,000 passengers who had put their trust in him, nor had he ever canceled a voyage; not even for a summer thunderstorm or early winter ice in the channel.

Running time was all-important. Every skipper wanted his boat to be the fastest. Marine architects attempted design after design in order to add a few minutes' speed. Captains risked collision or running aground in heavy fogs, or dodged and turned through the Highlands like a rabbit in front of hounds. Before the government erected range marks the captains and their assistants steered by any means at hand. At night they watched for notches in the mountain chains, little indentations that showed up against the lighter sky, or measured distances in their heads from one rocky outcropping to another. Good skippers claimed that they could tell how deep the channel was by the way the boat felt under their feet. With the growth in traffic, the lines operated both night boats and day boats to meet the needs of their various passengers. The night boats, favored by traveling salesmen eager to save time on their rounds, legislators on the way to the Albany State Capitol, and newlyweds, were marvelous sights from the shore: ablaze with lights, sparks shooting skyward from three and four stacks, and the foghorn blowing greetings at every landing. On pleasant summer nights all was jollity on board. When a thick fog settled on the river, blacking out both banks, the captain was sure to be found topside to "take her through."

One skipper did just that. The *Swallow*, steaming

downstream from Albany, was caught in a howling storm off Athens. It was April but a late snow had blanketed the river, hiding familiar landmarks. In the swirling snow the steamboat's captain saw what looked like the spars of two sailing vessels and steered between them—only to find, too late, that he was heading into a clutch of rocks with a few trees growing among them. He ordered the engines reversed, but nothing could save the *Swallow*. She ran full-tilt onto the shoal, "hog-backed," and broke in two. Residents of Athens hurried out to help, but fifteen lives were lost in the wreck. On charts of the Hudson that shoal today is marked as Swallow Rocks.

The Hudson saw many a steamboat race, some friendly and some bitter, as owners and captains sought to win or keep the speed record. The last and perhaps most famous was the one between the *Armenia* and the *Henry Clay*.

Captain Thomas Collyer had built the *Armenia* but had been forced to sell her to get money to complete the *Henry Clay*; and now that he was in the pilot house of the latter boat, every sight of the former enraged him. One day in July 1852, he was waiting to take aboard his passengers at the town of Hudson when he saw the other vessel going by downriver, passing up her regular stop. This goaded Collyer into action. Ordering the passengers to hurry, he cast off the *Clay*'s lines and headed out into midstream. James Elmendorf, pilot of the *Henry Clay*, warned Collyer he was risking trouble by ignoring the law against racing on the river. Collyer, furious, would not answer. When he did speak it was to order the safety valve tied down on the boilers. Pressure had built up to more than 350 pounds per square inch.

Hours later, Collyer inched his way abreast of the *Armenia*. Not content with a simple victory and driven by his mounting rage, he steered toward his rival until the guardrail of the *Clay* was under that of the *Armenia*. Then Collyer bellowed at the passengers to move to the far side. As the weight shifted the ships were locked and everyone knew that Collyer would drive the *Armenia* ashore if it did not lose speed. Isaac Polhemus, master of the threatened boat, sensed the danger, cut his en-

114

STEAMBOAT *Armenia*

The steamboat *Armenia*, as depicted in Volume I of the
G. W. Murdock Collection of Hudson River Steamboats.

BURNING OF THE STEAMBOAT *Henry Clay*

As the steamboats *Henry Clay* and *Armenia* raced south along the Hudson in July, 1852, the *Henry Clay* burst into flames; seventy-two persons were drowned or burned to death. This depiction of the tragedy is also taken from the Murdock Collection of Hudson River Steamboats.

gines, and allowed the *Armenia* to float free, losing much ground. The little victory did nothing to calm Collyer. He ordered his men to keep the safety valve tied down and raced along, ignoring the screams of frightened women, the crying of children, and the threats of angry male passengers. Finally, at Poughkeepsie, he grudgingly allowed those who wished to land to do so. Many stayed on.

Through the Highlands, past West Point, Stony Point, and into the broad reaches of Haverstraw Bay and the Tappan Zee, churned the *Henry Clay*. Behind, hopelessly beaten, steamed the *Armenia*. Then in mid-afternoon, as the boats thrashed past Yonkers, a stoker, his clothes ablaze, ran from the engine room and dived overboard. The fearful cry of "Fire!" swept through the *Henry Clay*. Flames enveloped the middle section of the boat, fanned by the wind created by the boat's swift passage. Elmendorf, the pilot, suggested beaching the *Clay* and, when Collyer, standing like a frozen statue in the wheelhouse, failed to reply, the pilot drove her ashore at Riverdale. Smokestacks, torn loose from their guywires, fell, sparks spread everywhere, and men, women, and children leaped overboard to escape the fire.

For Captain Collyer the final irony was the arrival of the *Armenia*. Seeing the disaster, Captain Polhemus came as close as he dared, put over his small boats and saved many of the passengers floundering frantically in the water. But seventy-two men, women, and children were beyond help—drowned or burned to death.

Chapter VI

The Time of the Barges

Metallurgy was still in its infancy when steamboating changed the life style of many along the Hudson River. Boilers had a nasty habit of blowing up, not only because captains were avid for new speed records but because science had not yet mastered the art of building great tensile strength into cast iron, sheet iron, and copper plating. Histories of the early days of steam are heavily larded with gruesome details of explosions that rocked boats, sent fire raging about the superstructure, and often forced passengers to leap overboard to escape the flames. Those early vessels were made of wood, decorated with gingerbread, and painted with highly combustible paints.

Native ingenuity found one way of lessening the danger, thus bringing greater peace of mind to many a passenger. The solution was the passenger "safety barge," a vessel built like the steamboat but without any engine room. It was towed along behind the steamboat, connected with a harness that reduced the vibrations of the towing craft and afforded more room for sleeping, dining, and promenading on the decks. Today the word "barge" usually evokes the ugly flatboats that carry railroad cars, cargo, and fuel around the waters of large ports. But the nineteenth-century Hudson River barges were altogether different: ornate, resplendent craft that drew admiring "oohs" and "ahs" from those on board as well as those along the river's banks.

119

PASSENGER BARGE *William H. Morton*

The wooden tow barge or "safety barge" *William H. Morton* was
built at Athens, New York, on the Hudson River, in 1854. Barges
of this type were chartered for passenger excursions during the
warmer months, and used in the transportation of freight during
the rest of the year. This oil painting by James Bard
(1815–1897), shows the barge being towed by the steamboat
America.

The Time of the Barges

With carpenters easy to find at less than $3 a day, these barges were built in a lavish style. Paneled walls, carpeted public rooms, huge French glass mirrors, ornate chandeliers, and massive furniture provided luxury and elegance unknown in all but the finest hotels. Most of the barges had two decks surmounted by an open promenade. The bottom level had staterooms or curtained berths along both sides, giving the passengers a clear view of the river. The doors opened into a central long room where dining tables were set with fine linen and cutlery. On the deck above were other staterooms, those reserved for the ladies, and a dressing room where gentlemen could shave and dress.

On pleasant days the promenade deck was the focal point of attraction: men and women sat on long settees facing the shores or strolled about to offset the gargantuan meals served in the dining saloon. From the steep escarpment of the Palisades to the level countryside near Albany each mile of travel brought new vistas of beauty. Sloops had by no means disappeared from the Hudson, but passengers on the steamboats and barges gloried no less in the scenery than had earlier travelers when wind was the propelling power. Many a steamer passenger would enthusiastically endorse Washington Irving's appraisal of the Catskills:

> But of all the scenery of the Hudson, the Kaatskill Mountains had the most witching effect on my boyish imagination. Never shall I forget the effect upon me of the first view of them predominating over a wide extent of country, part wild, woody, and rugged, part softened away into all the graces of cultivation. As we floated slowly along, I lay on the deck and watched them through a long summer's day; undergoing a thousand mutations under the magical effects of atmosphere, sometimes seeming to approach; at other times to recede; now almost melting into hazy distance, now burnished by the setting sun, until in the evening, they printed themselves against the glowing sky in the deep purple of an Italian landscape.

The Time of the Barges

Not all the passenger barges made the full trip between New York and Albany. Some were built expressly for local traffic and carried riders from Hudson and Catskill to Albany, or Poughkeepsie and Peekskill to New York, or on any of a number of short hauls. These barges were all ready, passengers and cargo on board, when a steamer came by, hooked up, and proceeded to convey them to their destination. The *Lady Clinton* was one of the first of the barges. Others included the *Lady Van Rensselaer*, *Charles Spear*, *Newburgh*, *Susquehanna*, *Walter Sands*, and *Caledonia*.

True, gentlemen were not allowed to sleep with their boots on, nor smoke "segars" in the public rooms, but travel by steamboat or "safety barge" was the fanciest and gayest of all travel in its time. The meals were unbelievable, and all evening long the band played waltzes, schottisches, and lancers for the young in heart. More than one tender romance blossomed between the piers of Manhattan and the docks in Albany.

Inevitably, time brought changes to the luxurious Hudson River safety barges. Steamers were built better and larger and boilers became safe. Eventually, with the sharpening competition some of the barges had to add cargo to make them profitable. So long as the freight consisted of dry goods, lumber, food, and grain, the situation remained tolerable; but with competition of railroads developing, the barges then began to carry livestock. With this change, the glory of the old days faded fast. For a while, some passengers put up with the bleating of sheep and the mooing of cattle, but before long even the most economy-minded persons opted for the steamboat to escape the noise and stench of goat pens and neighing horses.

For years, transporting horses from upstate New York down to New York City was a steady business. At the height of horse-car transportation in the city as many as three thousand horses were stabled at the barns where the cars were kept; so to keep the supply equal to the demand many horses had to be shipped downriver every month. As a result of these varying demands, more traffic moved on the Hudson in the first half of the nineteenth century than on any other river, and in the variety and number of craft that plied its waters the river was likewise without a peer.

The Marquis de Lafayette found the Hudson a place of wonder and beauty as well as progress when he made his triumphal tour of America in 1824. For this journey, the steamer *James Kent* was decorated with flags and bunting, filled with notables, and accompanied by scores of other craft on its run up the Hudson. On board were, among others, a granddaughter of George Washington, the widow and son of Alexander Hamilton, half the high officials of New York State and City and most of the members of the Society of the Cincinnati. The gala reception and dinner in the city on Tuesday evening had lasted until long after midnight, but, as Lafayette was anxious to visit West Point and other points of interest on the Hudson, the party went directly from dinner to the pier. The steamboat cast off at 2 A.M., Wednesday morning.

Some of the luminaries tried to snatch catnaps, but others watched the lights along the shore and listened to the firing of muskets and cannon honoring the French "hero of two worlds." All went well until the *James Kent* steamed into the Tappan Zee, where a dense fog came down off the hills and settled over the river. Off Tarrytown the decision was made to push on so as not to disappoint those waiting at the Military Academy. The fog worsened; the pilot could not even see the flagstaff on the bow of the steamboat. At seven in the morning when the sun should have burned away the mists, the *Kent* ignominiously ran aground on the Oyster Bank.

After several hours the tide came on to flood and the steamer was freed so that she could continue to West Point. That community was alive with people who had walked and ridden from the hinterland or sailed by sloop from towns along the river to welcome the Marquis. A contemporary, Frederick Butler, was almost carried away as he wrote of the scene;

> . . . at about fifteen minutes after 12, the welcome signal of his approach was given; and there was instantly more bustle and confusion than there has been before witnessed on the

Point since the army of the revolution; the clangour of arms, the thrilling notes of the bugle, and the spirit-stirring drum, imparted life and animation to this wild and magnificent region.—The lofty bank of the Hudson was lined with spectators; and the Cadets were in line, as if they had been summoned from their barracks by the wand of a magician.

After the tumultuous visit of Lafayette, life on the Hudson returned to normal. America was now on the move, and all classes traveled on the steamboats. Rough-looking laborers working on the Erie Canal rubbed elbows with horse traders and traveling salesmen as they devoured beefsteaks, buckwheat cakes, and similar plain, hearty fare.

Speed has always been a fetish and it was no less so in the earliest days of the steamboats. Often captains of the larger luxury steamers, eager to maintain fast schedules, devised clever ways of cutting down the landing time at intermediate points on the river. One of the most successful was to have a small boat towed by the steamer at the end of a long stout rope. As the steamer glided majestically past the small town the crew of the small boat would steer it to the pier, where passengers and their luggage were taken aboard. Meanwhile the rope was steadily played out from the steamboat. Once the passengers were seated, a signal was sent off and deckhands on the steamer, using a hand winch, pulled in the rope, drawing the small boat alongside the steamer. There another transfer was made without the steamer's having lost any appreciable time.

Americans were not the only ones who gloried in the floating palaces of the Hudson. Fanny Kemble, the noted English actress, had caustic words to say about American manners and dress, but she loved the steamboats. Mrs. Frances Trollope, Anthony's mother and herself a novelist, who had tried to recoup her family fortunes by running a drygoods store in Cincinnati, was even more vitriolic in her best-seller, *The Domestic Manners of the Americans* (1832), but she too was enamored of the Hudson's steamboats. Perhaps the biggest enthusiast of all was the English writer Harriet Martineau, who made three trips on

124

the Hudson for the simple reason that she enjoyed it. Her description will show why:

> I went three times up the Hudson; and, if I lived at New York, should be tempted to ascend it three times a week during the summer. Yet the greater number of ladies on board the steamboat remained in the close cabin among the crying babies, even while we were passing the finest scenery of the river. They do not share the taste of the gentleman who, when I was there, actually made the steamboat his place of abode during the entire summer season, sleeping on board at Albany and New York on alternate nights, and gazing at the shores all the day long with apparently undiminished delight. . . Farther on, the river widened into the Tappan Zee, and then the hills rose higher behind the banks, and wandering gleams lighted up a mountain region here and there.

Later on that trip she was introduced to Washington Irving, but the latter was rushing to catch a ferry to Cold Spring, and history has unfortunately not recorded their conversation. If there was time for anything other than the merest of pleasantries, it is most likely they both discussed the beauty of the river—a theme of which neither ever tired.

One of the delicacies served aboard was shad in season, for there was a time on the Hudson River when a person felt ashamed of himself if he did not have shad roe and bacon for breakfast almost every day from the middle of March to the beginning of June. If he did not catch the shad himself, he knew some fisherman who lived in a shanty on the edge of the river who had fish to spare.

Sometimes there would still be some ice floating on the river when the shad fishermen, their boats loaded down with slim oak or hickory poles, left home to set their nets. A mighty noise of hammering arose as they drove their poles down deep into the river silt. They would start just offshore and work their way out several hundred feet, making sure to stop short of the main channel. Within a few days, certain places on the river looked as if hundreds of backyards had been submerged by a flood with nothing but clothes poles showing above water. What the spectator could not see were long nets stretched from pole to pole, at right angles to the stream.

Not all those trying to catch shad used poles and nets. Fishing for shad is a little like politics in a two-party system, in which almost everyone belongs to one or the other party. But those who do not belong to either may be viewed with some suspicion. So for every man who stretches his net on poles, there is another who uses a drift net from a boat. The nets are made in the same way, with minor unimportant variations: they are woven with openings large enough for a shad's head to poke through, but too small for the curved, plumper body. Shad have big gill covers and, when they find they cannot go forward, they try to swim backwards and catch their gills in the nets.

Long before Henry Hudson sailed up the Hudson, the local Indians had been catching shad each spring. The Dutch pioneers lost no time in imitating their system. In the days of Peter Stuyvesant, nets were strung in the river as far down as Bayonne Point. However, increased shipping activity made that practice a precarious business, and in later times the first nets were put out from around Edgewater and West New York. Today, it is very rare to find a shad net below the George Washington Bridge. From the bridge north a traveler on the river can see rows of poles up to and sometimes a little beyond the Tappan Zee. In general, the drift netters, operating from boats, predominate above that point. Unquestionably, the largest commercial catches are made with stationary nets.

It is a curious anachronism to see tanned, wiry, and weather-beaten men tending their nets on a river that flows past large apartments and condominiums on the Palisades and the towering skyscrapers on Manhattan Island. But every spring, drawn by the lure of the catch, a small remnant of the old shad fishing fraternity turns to the Hudson again, their methods largely unchanged. Over the winter they have repaired their nets, readied new poles, one end sharpened to a stiletto point,

126

SHAD FISHERMEN ON THE SHORE OF THE HUDSON RIVER

Shad fishermen today tend their nets along the banks of the
Hudson much as they did in this nineteenth century painting by
Pavel Petrovich Svinin (1787–1839).

and reconditioned their outboard engines. By the end of March they are on the river, driving down the poles. This is no easy feat: a heavy cross-piece is harnessed to the pole and two men stand on it, one on each side of the pole. At a shouted command, they jump into the air and then land back on the cross-piece with all their weight. This goes on—the men substituting for a pile driver—until the pole is solidly anchored in the river silt. As soon as the first shad start up the river to spawn, the men are out in their boats, hanging nets from the poles. Twice a day until late in April, they drape the nets along about twelve hundred feet of poles at ebb tide; and twice a day, when the tide comes on full, they lift the nets, plucking the fish from their nets as vintners pick grapes from the vines.

Farther upstream the drift-net men have not been idle. Their boats are ready and their nets, with weights at the bottom and floats at the top, are folded neatly in the stern. Word spreads quickly and there is an audible alarm that moves north upriver with the first of the shad: "The silverbacks are running!" The fishermen let the nets out slowly as they row along the shore, staying away from the deep channel in the middle. By watching the floats, which bob up and down when shad are trapped in the net nearby, they know when it is time to pull in the seine. No matter how the nets are used, it is hard work to get the shad into the boats, which must be kept in the right position regardless of wind, tide, or the wakes created by passing freighters and barges. Fingers grow numb, backs ache, and the blood chills from continued exposure.

To the shad this is all part of their vast, awesome life cycle, of which the Hudson itself is an integral part. Four or five years before, a female shad swam upstream to the flats between Kingston and Coxsackie, her body heavy with eggs, or roe. There she deposited the eggs, numbering anywhere from one hundred thousand to four hundred thousand, on the river bottom, where they were fertilized by the milt of the male, or buck shad. Despite those staggering figures, probably fewer than a dozen of those eggs matured into grown fish. Most were eaten by predators, damaged by storms, or destroyed by chemical pollution.

128

The tiny survivors spent the summer on the upper Hudson until the weather turned cold, when they headed for the open ocean. Small and defenseless, they were still the prey of many larger species as they spent the next four years roaming off the Continental Shelf.

When they passed the skyscrapers of Manhattan on their way out of the river, they were still only from three to five inches in length. Four or five years later, weighing an average of two to five pounds, but sometimes heavier, they answered a mysterious call from the upper Hudson. In large schools they swam back to New York harbor, up the Narrows, past the steel and glass towers, through the Highlands, and finally to the broader reaches of the stream where life had begun for them.

The first shad to move upriver to spawn tend to run smaller than those that come later. Iridescent and shiny, they were given the nickname of "silverbacks" generations ago. The swallows that return to Capistrano in California each spring may be more romantic, but when the silverbacks start running, thousands along the Hudson respond excitedly to the migration.

Statistics can make for dull reading, hence a minimum of figures will suffice here. In 1889, the Hudson catch amounted to 4,332,000 pounds—the all-time record. By 1916, when the all-time low record was set, a mere 40,000 pounds, it seemed that the noble shad was doomed. But during World War II the number rose to almost equal the 1889 figure. Ichthyologists have debated the reasons for the wide variations without, however, arriving at a consensus. Driven by fear that someday the shad would disappear from the Hudson, government authorities limited drift nets to 2,000 feet in length, to give the migrating fish enough room to pass through. Then they ruled that all nets must be lifted from the river from Friday morning until Sunday morning.

Wise fishermen caught as many silverbacks as they could at the beginning of the season, all the while looking forward to the time when the season neared its end. Then the "lilacs" came upstream, big shad running up to twelve and thirteen pounds for a female with roe. The "lilacs," so-called because by then the lilacs were in bloom beside the river, were the aristocrats of the shad migration. When the gill nets were heavy with "lilacs" there was joy in the hearts of commercial shad fishermen.

Writing about shad tends to call forth the past tense, for nowadays the catch is nothing like what it was. Each year the fishermen of Edgewater and Alpine hint that the next season may be their last. However, local politicians still go to Washington and argue with the Corps of Engineers to keep channels open and prevent the passage of any regulations that would further hamper the dwindling number of fishermen still active each spawning season. For decades their unofficial headquarters was the Colonial Tavern, almost two miles south of the Jersey end of the George Washington Bridge. The building stood in the midst of decaying barges, small boatyards, and canoe and rowing clubs. The old-timers formed the Hudson River Shad Fishermen's Association to defend their rights in a rapidly changing world.

Many assert that shad fishing is doomed. However, the cycle may simply be at a low point. One day the shad may be back in the numbers that amazed the first Dutch settlers. Old-timers along the river say that when the young fry swam down the Hudson in the fall, heading for the ocean depths, there were so many of them and they swam so close to the surface, that from the shore and the bridges that span the river it looked as if it were raining.

Shadbakes are among the most colorful of old American customs. Well before the crowd arrives, the people in charge have gathered plenty of hard wood—it makes the best embers—and cleaned hundreds of the fish. The wood is ignited early in the day to get rid of most of the smoke and to form a good bed of red-hot coals about twenty feet long and a yard across. The halves of shad, or fillets, glistening white, are pegged onto inch-thick oak boards about the size of a child's writing tablet. Across the fillets are draped two or three slices of lean bacon. As soon as the guests arrive, the planks are set around the bed of coals, tilted just enough to keep the fish from slipping off. The intense heat reflected from the fire sets the bacon to sizzling and the fat

130

bastes the fillets. Every once in a while the boards are upended to brown the fish evenly. Over another bed of embers roe is cooking in shallow skillets. The meal commences with clam chowder, but as soon as the bowls are removed, the shad and roe are served, sometimes with a salad and sometimes with corn on the cob. A participant who doesn't ask for a second helping doesn't deserve to go to a shadbake. The urge to attend one is almost as strong as the one that brings the shad back each spring to renew their life cycle.

Chapter VII

The Erie Canal

Like a massive barricade, the Appalachian mountain range hemmed in the early settlers of North America, confining them to the lowlands along the sea. From the Gaspé peninsula to central Alabama, it lay athwart their expansion to the west. Getting through the mountains preoccupied several generations of Americans. Some hoped that the Potomac would provide access to the interior, but that stream petered out in the high mountains of western Virginia. The James River route ended at the Blue Ridge, and the Susquehanna-Juniata system was no solution, leaving travelers in the foothills of the Alleghenies with a hundred miles still to go before reaching a tributary of the Ohio River.

But nature had left one break in the barrier which, without being aware of it, Henry Hudson had discovered. Over the ages, the waters of the Mohawk, joining those of the upper Hudson, had cut a channel, splitting apart the Highlands only fifty miles from the ocean, creating what was virtually a water-level route from the Atlantic to the Great Lakes and the wellsprings of the Mississippi.

During the French and Indian War (1754–1763), Washington would have welcomed an easier route to the junction of the rivers that formed the Ohio at Fort Pitt, for he was fully cognizant of the advantages of traveling along natural waterways. The year the Revolutionary War ended, he made an extended tour of the Hudson, Mohawk, and Oneida Lake route to Lake Ontario; the following year he proposed to Congress that it extend inland navigation wherever possible, including a route in New York leading to Lake Erie. Before a decade had passed, companies were formed and work was actively progressing on canals to link the Hudson and Lake Champlain and the Mohawk and Lake Ontario.

There were New York State citizens with sufficient vision to see that a long canal tying the Hudson to Lake Erie would be of significant use. De Witt Clinton, General Philip Schuyler, George Tibbetts, and Martin Van Buren were among those who supported the bills passed authorizing construction of such a canal. Despite arguments over contracts, delays over engineering techniques, political bribery and chicanery, the project advanced. Finally, on July 4, 1817, scores of top-hatted officials gathered in the upstate town of Rome, shovels in hand, waiting for the sun to rise. When the first golden rays pierced the mist at the eastern horizon, cannon boomed, people shouted, and the dignitaries drove their shovels into the rich earth beside the Mohawk. The Erie Canal had become a reality; there was nothing left now but the actual construction work.

It took eight years to finish the job. Legend has it that Irish immigrants did the hard work, but official records tell a somewhat different story. More than 75 percent of the workmen were native New Yorkers, eager to earn fifty cents a day. With horse and scraper, oxen and heavy drays, they dug through earth, blasted through rock, pushed trestles across swamps, erected aqueducts to supply water, and built locks and dams. West of Syracuse the canal was like a magic wand conjuring up new towns, luring settlers, opening up what was still a vast, undeveloped land. Along the Hudson, it was a promise that the riches of the west would pass through New York State instead of down the Canadian St. Lawrence. The "Big Ditch" seemed to be all things to all men. Albany worried a little lest its port lose its longtime importance and New York City grow too powerful; but as cargo started moving along the canal it soon became apparent that there would be commerce enough for everyone.

ENTRANCE OF THE ERIE CANAL INTO THE HUDSON AT ALBANY, 1824

Part of the system of locks which accommodated the differing water levels along the route is shown in this engraving of the junction of the Erie Canal and the Hudson River at Albany. The original illustration is from Eaton's Geological Survey, 1824

The Erie Canal

From 1825, when it was completed, until long after the Civil War, the Erie Canal carried the lifeblood of a considerable part of the nation. To be sure, by today's standards, it was not a big canal: only forty feet wide at the top and only four feet deep; but it was 363 miles long. Lake Erie at Buffalo, where the canal terminated in the west, is 565 feet higher than the Hudson at Albany; but this was only one of several reasons for a system of locks. There were numerous differences in elevation due to hills and valleys between Buffalo and Albany. All told, the canal had eighty-three locks with lifts of from six to twelve feet and eighteen aqueducts to bring water from nearby rivers or to carry the canal itself across deep valleys. Understandably, the young nation took pride in this outstanding engineering feat.

Its completion was the signal for New York State to explode with joy, to "strike the lyre and beat the drum," and celebrate in an unprecedented excess of patriotism and pride. During weeks of unalloyed excitement, every town, on or away from the canal, sought to outdo the others in heralding the great event.

The central celebration began when the towboat *Seneca Chief*, with Governor Clinton, Chancellor Robert Livingston, Stephen Van Rensselaer, and other luminaries on board, set out toward the east from Buffalo. In midmorning of October 26, 1825, Jesse Hawley, one of the commissioners, extravagantly told the notables on the towboat that New York had "made the longest canal—in the least time—with the least experience—for the least money—and of the greatest public utility of any other in the world."

The *Seneca Chief* was a sight to behold. Strewn with flags and bunting, its main cabin boasted a portrait of Clinton garbed in a Roman toga, painted by the talented George Catlin. Under careful guard were various bits of cargo of no great intrinsic value but much more important than they seemed: two wooden kegs of "the pure water of Lake Erie," red cedar and birdseye maple logs with which to make commemorative medals, whitefish from the lakes, grain from the west, and even a birchbark canoe fashioned by Indians on the shore of faraway Lake Superior.

136

The Erie Canal

As De Witt Clinton watched the sides of the canal glide by, a 32-pounder fired an opening salute. Immediately, another gun to the east fired its charge and so it went until the signal had reached Sandy Hook in New York harbor, to be relayed back along the canal. It took three hours and twenty minutes for the "Grand Salute" to go from Buffalo to New York and back. Behind the lead boat, towed effortlessly by stout horses or mules, came others in the official party: the *Noah's Ark*, the *Niagara*, the *Black Rock*, and the *Superior*, bearing besides the dignitaries such odds and ends as a gentle fawn, birds, insects, and animals of the Great Lakes region, and two young Seneca Indian boys.

At every lock, at every town, the procession was feted with speeches, banquets, fireworks, and tableaus. Clinton was hailed as a conquering hero and the canal engineers were accorded only slightly lower status. At Rochester the boats were joined by the *Young Lion of the West* on board which were cages of wolves, raccoons, foxes, deer, and other animals native to the area. On Tuesday evening the flotilla was in Rochester, on Saturday it was in Syracuse, and by Sunday it had reached Utica in time for church services. On Monday it passed Little Falls, Tuesday saw it welcomed by the students at Union College in Schenectady, and on Wednesday morning, almost a week to the hour after the Buffalo departure, the little party of towboats was locked down into the boat basin at Albany.

If there had been fears that Albany would lose prominence because of the canal, they were dispelled when the *Seneca Chief* tied up. The capital city outdid all others along the route of the canal, providing fireworks, parades, reviews, banquets, and speeches until it must have seemed that the entire city wanted to proclaim the wonders of modern transportation.

When the main welcome was offered in the Assembly chamber, the portraits of three great Americans looked down from the walls: George Washington, George Clinton, and, as if he had not won honors enough, De Witt Clinton. All the celebrating was packed into that one day and evening, because the people in charge of the event had momentous plans for the morrow. At ten o'clock the next morning, November 3, the canal

DEWITT CLINTON

De Witt Clinton, Governor of New York at the time of the
completion of the Erie Canal, from a painting by Alonzo
Chappell (1828–1877), originally published in 1861.

boats began the last lap of their auspicious voyage, down the Hudson to the Atlantic. Somewhere on the outskirts of Albany the horses and mules that had pulled the canal boats across the state were put out to pasture for a day or so. From there on in, the *Seneca Chief* and the other curious-looking little boats would be towed by river steamers. The *Chancellor Livingston*, aflutter with flags, was given the honor of towing the *Chief*. The *Constitution*, which had just won the blue ribbon for fastest time on the Hudson, was assigned to the *Young Lion*, and the *Chief Justice Marshall* put out lines to the *Niagara*. Behind them steamed the *Constellation*, the *Swiftsure*, and the *Olive Branch*, towing the safety barges *Matilda* and *Richmond*.

With flawless precision the flotilla moved off from the port of Albany, cannon booming behind them and shouts echoing and re-echoing across the river where Kiliaen Van Rensselaer had established his patroonship nearly two centuries before. The naval parade was one long tribute to the builders of the Erie Canal. Bonfires burned on the hillsides, militia companies fired fusillades, and every passing vessel rang its bell, tooted its horn, or dipped a flag at the colorful armada. One by one, the towns of Athens, Hudson, Catskill, Saugerties, and Kingston dropped astern as the unusually warm November afternoon turned to evening. The advent of darkness was a signal for the steamboats to dress ship with gleaming lanterns, transforming the procession into a moving fairyland of twinkling lights. Along the river banks, farmers and fishermen, tanners and carpenters gathered to view the spectacle. Around midnight the *Chancellor Livingston* briefly dropped anchor off West Point so the cadet band could come aboard and serenade the passengers.

At seven o'clock the next morning, as the bells in all the church steeples of New York City pealed out their welcome, a deputation from the city government, on board the steamboat *Washington*, met the line of ships from Albany. Rounding the Battery, the flotilla steamed to the Brooklyn Navy Yard for a formal salute, then returned to start the water parade to Sandy Hook. One after another, other vessels joined the procession: Hudson River steamers, transatlantic packets, the revenue cutter *Alert*, the steamer *Fulton*, given a place of honor because of her name, and many others. The sailing packet *Hamlet*, her sails sagging in the absence of even a feeble wind, was taken in tow as the "Grand Aquatic Display" passed out of the Upper Bay, through the Narrows where guns boomed again from the forts guarding the city, and on into the bay behind Sandy Hook. The *U.S.S. Porpoise*, a schooner assigned as "a Deputation from Neptune," was waiting there. Wheeling neatly on the calm waters behind the sandy spit with its tall lighthouse, the vessels took up stations in a large circle three miles around.

The men who had planned and built the canal would have preferred to see the ceremonies, officially labeled "The Wedding of the Waters," performed on the deck of the *Seneca Chief*. But officialdom had its way, and the notables all transferred to the steamer *Washington*. From the canal boats they took the two kegs of "pure" Lake Erie water and from other vessels they carried bottles and phials filled many months ago from other seas and rivers around the world.

Governor Clinton, straining at the unusual chore, lifted one of the kegs and poured the water from the Great Lakes into the Atlantic. As he prepared to empty the other cask, someone hit upon the brilliant idea of saving some water to be sent to General Lafayette, not only to honor the elderly Marquis for his role in the War of Independence, but because he had taken time on his recent tour to ride in a boat on a portion of the unfinished canal in the western part of the state. Because he had saved his speech for the second cask, the governor poured a little from that one over the side, saying as he did so, "May the God of the heavens and the earth smile most propitiously on this work, accomplished by the wisdom, public spirit, and energy of the people of the State of New York." Enough of the water was left to carry out the plan to send some to Lafayette in bottles manufactured in the United States and packed in a box made by Duncan Phyfe out of one of the cedar logs carried all the way from Buffalo on the *Seneca Chief*.

Next, the smaller bottles and phials, one by one, were opened by the chief speaker, Dr. Samuel Latham Mitchill, and

Museum of the City of New York

ERIE CANAL CELEBRATION, NOVEMBER 4, 1825

Vessels of all sorts sailed down the Hudson to New York City for the grand
celebration of the completion of the Erie Canal, shown here in a steel
engraving (c. 1825), by J. L. Morton (1792–1871).

KEG OF LAKE ERIE WATER FROM ERIE CANAL CELEBRATION

From this keg, Governor De Witt Clinton poured water from Lake Erie into the Atlantic. Some of the water from the Great Lakes was also saved and later sent to the Marquis de Lafayette, who had traveled on a portion of the canal during a visit before its completion.

their contents poured into the salty Atlantic. There was water from the Nile, where Cleopatra's barge had carried her to meet Mark Anthony, water from the sacred Ganges, from the mighty Amazon, the Seine at Paris, the Elbe, Tagus, Danube, Gambia, Orinoco, and Columbia; even from the Neva in far-off Russia.

As if "The Wedding of the Waters" were not ritual enough to mark the canal's completion, the thousands on shore who had not witnessed the ceremony at Sandy Hook got a parade featuring woodsmen carrying axes to show how the wilderness had been won, tailors, printers, clothiers, chandlers, millers, bakers, butchers, and a host of other tradesmen and artisans. Some simply marched along, content to carry their banners; not so the carpenters and the combmakers. Working at a furious pace on a horse-drawn platform, the carpenters displayed their expertise by making a sixty-gallon cask—and then a smaller one to show they were not tired. But it was the combmakers who stole the show. As their float moved along Greenwich, Canal, and Broome Streets and lower Broadway, they cut out, polished, and tossed to female watchers along the route fifty dozen shell and horn combs.

That night there was a fireworks display at City Hall that was talked about for over a century—until the Philadelphia Sesquicentennial of 1926. New Yorkers were also busy looking at the animals in the cages on *Noah's Ark*, the canal boat tied up at Castle Garden, or marveling at the two Seneca Indian boys, resplendent in native costume. A little farther uptown, another crowd waited impatiently for daring Madame Johnson to make a balloon ascent. When her helpers could not fill the craft with gas, the crowd became enraged, demanded the return of their fifty-cent admission fees, and, when this was refused, tore the balloon to shreds. Then they proceeded to the methodical destruction of Vauxhall Gardens. When the merrymakers had had their fill of speeches, banquets, parades, and fireworks, the canal boats started back up the Hudson. This time the *Seneca Chief* carried a keg filled with water from the ocean, to be dumped into Lake Erie. In all the excitement there had been but one mishap: two men loading a cannon at Weedsport had been blown to bits when the old field piece burst during a salute to the passing parade.

Once the excitement was over, the canal became a busy waterway. New boats were built in a dozen yards, horses and mules were purchased all over the east and in Canada to do the towing, and as many as five thousand boys found employment as drivers. People from the larger cities along the coast, reading eloquent handbills of the big land companies, started west along the canal to seek their fortunes. Old world immigrants by the thousands followed in their tracks. The foreigners had to endure the same travail at the Buffalo terminus of the canal that early steamboat travelers had experienced in New York City.

Many of the immigrants found that travel on the canal was scarcely better than the transatlantic crossing in a cattle boat, yet the tide swept on. There were outbreaks of cholera and smallpox, deaths and burials along the towpaths, but nothing could halt the movement toward the west.

Within a few years after the first settlers had claimed new farms in Ohio, Michigan, and Illinois, wheat, corn, barley, oats, lumber, and other produce started east to tidewater. By 1852, down-canal traffic brought to the Albany basin more than a million tons of cargo; and as commerce grew, so did the city, which quadrupled in population in the twenty-six years after the grand opening in 1825. Albany was not only an inland port, it was a busy seaport. Some of the produce brought there by canal was sent down the Hudson in giant tows of fifty or a hundred boats lashed together behind a single steamboat. Other cargo was transferred out of the canal boats into steamboats, sloops, and schooners. The steamboat was king of the river but the sloop too was still very much alive.

During the season when the Erie Canal was open, Albany port records in 1843 show the arrival or departure of 33 steamboats and 64 steam towboats—and 2,470 sloops and schooners. As Albany grew in size and wealth, so did the metropolis at the mouth of the Hudson. Every river town along the Hudson benefited in a multitude of ways from the building of the canal, as did those along the inland waterway itself. Fortunes were

145

ALBANY

The lithograph of the city of Albany from the Hudson, on page 145, included in Jacques Milbert's *Picturesque Itinerary of the Hudson River,* published in 1828–29, reflects what Albany would have looked like about the time of the opening of the Erie Canal in 1825. Within the next twenty years, the amount of marine traffic in Albany increased dramatically, as did the city's population.

made because of it, towns were created to serve it, and history was shaped by it.

Henry Hudson would have enjoyed seeing the heavy traffic on the Erie Canal and the Hudson River when the canal was in its heyday. True, it didn't reach to Cathay, but was, in its own way, a Northwest Passage of great importance.

More than one poor man used it as his ladder to success, as, for example, an Irish lad whose family migrated to New York in 1850. The boy, Michael Moran, trudged the towpaths for fifty cents a day, six hours on and six hours off. Later he served as a tillerman on a boat, saved his money, and bought a boat of his own. Before he had been in the United States ten years he had amassed a fleet of boats and went on to form the Moran Towing Corporation, today the world's largest of its kind. More than 125 years have passed and towboats with his family name on them still plow the waters of the canal, the Hudson, and even the deep-sea lanes of the world.

The opening of the Erie Canal changed the face of the Hudson River Valley—in agriculture, industry, and social patterns of living. America's new frontier was now pushed far to the west, where fertile farmland was abundantly available; so hundreds of thousands took up the trek westward. As for the Valley itself, more than one historian speaks of a "Yankee Invasion," for many of the new settlers crossed over from New England, especially Connecticut and Massachusetts.

With cheaper lands beckoning in the West, marked changes in agriculture and industry occurred in the Hudson Valley. Where before wheat growing and flour milling had prospered, particularly around the town of Catskill, these occupations were transferred farther west. By 1840, Rochester had become the leading flour-milling center in the United States. Likewise the tanning industry, utilizing the giant hemlock trees of the Catskills, lost the importance it had acquired in the first decades of the nineteenth century under such hard-driving entrepreneurs as Colonel William Edwards and Colonel Zadock Pratt. Instead, the newcomers to the Hudson Valley planted corn and produced excellent crops on the floodplains of the tributary streams, the Esopus and Walkill. Dairy farming expanded noticeably and still plays a significant role in the economy of the Hudson Valley region today. The versatile Andrew Jackson Downing and his brother Charles, born in Newburgh, pioneered in replacing wheat with fruit crops—apples, pears, grapes, and plums—on the west bank of the Hudson in the Highlands region. To this day the area around Highland, Clintondale, and New Paltz is noted for its high-quality apples, many of which are exported to Europe.

In industry too there were noteworthy changes. Brickmaking and cement, benefiting from an abundant supply of locally quarried materials, remained mainstays of the region's economy; but a newcomer, textiles, soon came to the fore. Cotton cloth and knit goods were manufactured in Cohoes; Troy became the national center of the collar and shirt industry. It is no exaggeration to characterize the Hudson Valley's growth after the opening of the Erie Canal as an industrial revolution. By 1850 New York State, with three million inhabitants, had more population than any other two states combined. In industrial production it led the nation.

The need for free labor, increasingly urgent, was met in part by the Yankee invasion mentioned above, but even more so by a sharp increase in European immigration. Large numbers of Irish and Germans came, particularly after the abortive 1848 revolution in Germany and the "potato famine" in Ireland. The Irish soon became the predominant labor force in two of the most physically demanding occupations: brickmaking and cement work. As the century drew to a close, of course, the stream of immigrants was to become a flood.

A smaller but no less notable accretion was from the recently emancipated black slaves. Slavery had hung on longer in New York than in other northern states. A gradual emancipation began in 1799, but complete freedom was not proclaimed until 1827, when it was codified in New York's Constitution.

By the time William Seward became governor (1839–1842), New York State was irrevocably in the antislavery camp. Seward himself, who was to serve as Lincoln's wartime Secretary of

State, became an uncompromising foe of slavery in the years before the Civil War. His Rochester speech of 1858, warning about
the "irrepressible conflict," reverberated throughout the land.
John Brown, taking up residence in 1849 in North Elba town-
ship in Essex County, was actively engaged in the Underground
Railroad from his wilderness home. Towns farther south, such as
Troy, Albany, and Poughkeepsie, participated in this historic
movement to spirit fugitive southern slaves to freedom in the
northern United States and Canada. The favorite route was up
the Hudson to Albany; then it split into two forks: one above
Troy and into Vermont, up the Champlain Valley to Canada, the
other west through Utica and Syracuse to Lockport and Niagara.

For more than a century the Hudson River Valley owed a
great deal to Frederick Tudor, a New England Yankee, whose
business foresight revolutionized winter life for thousands of
York State men. Tudor decided the world could use ice in the
summertime. After persuading Bostonians to buy his product,
he took a shipload to Havana where, although half of his cargo
melted on the way, he turned a handsome profit. Boston became
the "Ice Port" of America, and people living in cold climates
sawed, picked, and shoveled ice in emulation of Boston's
success.

Residents of New York, Brooklyn, Jersey City, and other
large communities at the mouth of the Hudson saw no reason
why their lemonade should not be ice-cold in July or their meat
kept wholesome in August. So the ice-cutting and ice-storing industry boomed upriver. By the end of the Civil War approximately three million tons of ice were harvested every winter on
the upper Hudson and adjacent lakes.

In most of the places north of Kingston, good, solid ice
started forming soon after Christmas. When it reached twelve or
fourteen inches in thickness men appeared on the glassy surface
as if by magic, carrying saws, tongs, planers, chisels, icehooks,
and axes. Lines were marked on the ice and horse-drawn plows
with special cutting flanges followed along, gouging a deep cut
which was finished by men with long handsaws. Very soon long

channels were full of bobbing cakes of ice that were poled toward shore. It was exacting work. If the ice cakes were not kept in motion they would freeze together and close the channel. If it snowed, as it usually did, horse-drawn scrapers had to be used to remove the snow, as snow ice melts too fast. Moreover, people did not like their ice to look cloudy. One company boasted that you could read a newspaper through a twenty-inch block of its ice.

Ice cutting was a precarious enterprise, economically and physically. For the entrepreneur, a sudden thaw or rainstorm could ruin a harvest. For the worker, a misstep could lead to a plunge into bitterly cold water, usually resulting in pneumonia even if the man was pulled out quickly. And death was the result if the current in the river sucked the victim under the ice. Cutting ice was also a backbreaking job. Inventors perfected circular saws powered by steam, but the apparatus was so heavy it broke through all but the thickest of ice. By the time the internal-combustion engine was improved, bringing ample power and lightweight equipment to the river and lakes, the production of artificial ice had begun and eventually the industry moved indoors, away from frozen ponds and rivers. (But this was not to occur until after the First World War.)

In the nineteenth century harvesting ice in New York State was part hard work, part gamble, and part romance. Artists painted numerous scenes of ice cutting on the frozen expanses of river and lakes. Currier & Ives sold millions of lithographs on that subject. But a cake of ice on the upper Hudson in February had little value; the challenge was to preserve it until the next summer when people would pay for it. This meant that ice had to be stored.

All along the shore of the river north of the Highlands—mostly on the western side—there developed hundreds of huge, barn-sized, ice houses. Using nothing but wood, the builders of these structures achieved an amazing degree of control over the inside temperature. The buildings had an outer skin of cheap pine sheathing and an inner wall, usually of hemlock. Sawdust was dumped into the spaces between these walls, thus

ICE-GATHERING ON THE HUDSON RIVER

This illustration of the process of ice-gathering on the Hudson River is from the March 27, 1875, issue of *Scientific American*.

providing an excellent insulating material. Each year the best-run storage houses were painted a bright white to reflect as much of the sun's heat as possible. Some houses consisted of a single room, but larger ones were divided into separate rooms, each one holding about ten thousand tons of ice. On the side facing the river or lake narrow doorways ran from the ground up to the eaves and inclined ramps stretched from the water's edge to the openings. Up these ramps the blocks of ice were towed, some by block and falls powered by a horse, or, in later years, on an endless chain powered by steam engines.

At the height of the harvest the glittering bluish-white cakes of ice were poled out of the river channel onto the lower end of the inclined ramp and carried in an unending stream into the dark caverns of the storage houses. There they were piled in rows, leaving room for air circulation, and then covered with sawdust. As the ice level inside the building mounted, the ramp was tilted higher and higher until the house was filled. Then the doorways were battened down. Up under the roof, the loft of the building was filled with salt hay, sawdust, or shavings to insulate against the summer's sunshine. The more efficient companies achieved such success that the meltage loss was kept under 20 percent until the time came for the ice to be shipped down the Hudson to the metropolis. Most firms counted on approximately 50 percent loss during the winter storage, the forwarding to market, and the distribution to individual homes and businesses in the city.

What worried the ice companies the most were "open" winters. Every three or four years, the Hudson would not freeze until late in January and then might attain a thickness of little more than six or seven inches. When this happened, cutters, horses, wagons, and tools rushed upriver beyond Albany and to Lake Champlain to find better ice. Big firms, such as the Knickerbocker Ice Company and Consumers Ice Company, could contract for supplies in Canada and Maine, but the smaller ones found that last year's profits would not cover this year's losses. Knickerbocker and Consumers were the two giants in the industry. A list of locations where they harvested ice reads like

THE KNICKERBOCKER COMPANY CUTTING ICE

The Knickerbocker Ice Company, one of the two largest in the state, cut ice not only on the Hudson River, but also on nearby Rockland Lake. From there, cakes of ice were transported to the Hudson to be loaded onto barges.

an enumeration of most of the Hudson River towns. Nor did they limit their operations to the river itself; they took large quantities of ice from Rockland, Kensico, Greenwood, and Highland Lakes. Knickerbocker Ice operated not only storage houses but also farms to raise feed for the horses and hay for packing the ice, as well as machine shops to keep equipment in repair. At Rockland it operated a small railroad and an inclined plane over the summit of the mountain, in order to reach the Hudson where the barges were loaded.

These barges, specifically built for the purpose, helped swell the traffic on the river every summer. They ranged from 110 to 140 feet in length and from 300 to 750 tons deadweight, one of the larger ones easily carrying 1,000 tons at a time. Builders had no eye for beauty; they made their barges blunt at bow and stern with cargo houses on the main deck so that they looked like awkward houseboats without windows. Hundreds of them could be seen loading at West Camp, Athens, New Baltimore, Rondout, Coxsackie, Castleton, and other small towns in between. Some were lashed together in fleets of ten or a dozen and towed downstream by steam tugs. Each barge had a small windmill on the cargo-house roof that drove a pump which cleared the hold of water from melting ice. With a bit of imagination, one could mistake a fleet of these craft for a small cluster of houses moving along a Dutch canal.

Once the ice reached the depots along the waterfront in New York City, everyone connected with the industry engaged in a frenzied effort to beat the heat. In the old days, wagons were loaded inside the ice depots to avoid the bright summer sun, and the drivers often gave the horses the whip to reach their route areas more quickly. The minute an ice wagon drove into a neighborhood, the youngsters swarmed around, hoping to find chips of ice broken off as the drivers cut blocks to fit individual iceboxes. The more daring were not content to look. Waiting until the deliveryman went inside a house, a block of ice slung over his shoulder, they swiftly hacked away at the supply kept under the wet blankets and old rugs to obtain their own chips. The deliveryman knew what size chunk the lady of the house wanted because a card hung in the window or on a nail by the door indicated the number of pounds to be brought in. With nothing but his icepick or one claw of his tongs, an experienced iceman could cut off a piece that would not weigh a pound under or over the desired size. In earlier days, back doors were usually left open for the iceman. The icebox was a simple affair of wood lined with zinc or galvanized iron; it had a chamber for ice in the top, and below, another with shelves for food, to take advantage of the fact that cold air descends.

During the period when natural ice constituted the bulk of the supply in New York City, records indicate that at least seven hundred wagons were constantly busy distributing it throughout the city. Stables for the teams were almost as numerous as those for the horsecars, brewery wagons, and bakery carts. But then a swift decline set in. First, the manufacture of artificial ice doomed the natural-ice business on the upper Hudson; then the gas and electric refrigerator supplanted the breweries that had gone into the ice-making business during the Prohibition era.

On the river, ice harvesting became a thing of the past. The big storage houses crumbled into ruins, although a few were used, for a time, for cultivating mushrooms. The barges disappeared and the small shipyards on the river's banks fell on hard days. But, by this time, the railroads had already largely turned ice-shipping by barges into an anachronism—a colorful carry-over from times gone by.

Chapter VIII

The Iron Horse

Even in the heyday of the elegant steamboats on the Hudson their doom was being spelled out, just a few yards in from the river banks. A long pier jutting out into the lower Tappan Zee connected the tracks of the Erie Railroad with the landing wharves of passenger and freight steamers; and to the east, following the valleys between the Taconic Mountains and the ridges along the Hudson, trains ran on the tracks of the New York and Harlem line. From the decks of the steamers one could not see the trains, except on the Piermont levee, but they were there, threatening both the canals and the steamship lines. The reasons for their competitive advantage was speed and their ability to run even while the river and canals froze up for at least a third of the year.

Consider, for example, the winter of 1831. Autumn had been fairly mild and the steamers kept on running, hoping against a hard freeze. Then from out of the northwest came bitter winds and low temperatures. At Poughkeepsie and several other landings the freight boats were loaded to the gunwales with Dutchess County beef and pork, destined for New York City. But before the crews could get up steam, the boats were frozen in solid. Thereupon a hue and cry arose, led by Matthew Vassar, the Poughkeepsie brewer. Vassar informed his fellow businessmen about the New York and Harlem, then inching its way up-state a few miles each week, and asked pointedly why the river towns did not have a railroad of their own. Nor did the citizens feel easier when a local paper printed a piece of doggerel about the boatloads of pork, still rotting at the waterfront:

> *Railroads are all the rage of latter years*
> *They talk of one to go from here to York,*
> *To quell the city people's anxious fears*
> *And carry down the Dutchess County pork.*
> *The cars are wondrous things to load our trash on,*
> *And tho' our boatmen starve, 'twill be in fashion.*

By 1842, a committee, active for several years, appealed to the state legislature for a railroad charter. The entrenched steamboat interests gathered at Albany, predicting dire things if the railroad was authorized, and lobbied successfully to have the idea rejected. Three years later, however, another meeting was held, this time at New York University in the metropolis, resulting in action by the legislature. A charter was obtained, subscriptions poured in, and gangs of workmen began building the New York & Hudson Railroad, which was to run up along the river, from Chambers and Hudson Streets to Greenbush, across the river from Albany.

In Manhattan the tracks—a double set—went right along the riverbank, cutting across the front lawns of many well-to-do suburbanites then living in Manhattanville and Inwood. Two awards totaling $3,000 were paid to John James Audubon for this intrusion, $800 went to the elderly Madame Jumel, and other payments were made to placate their neighbors. When the tracks reached Tarrytown, Washington Irving was cajoled by his friend Gouverneur Kemble not to stand in the way of progress. After receiving company stock, Irving granted the line permission to cut across his land; but he soon came to regret his decision because of the din from the engines and cars and the fumes from the smokestacks.

By October 1849, trains were running from New York to a point above Peekskill. The locomotives looked like overgrown teakettles and the cars were not much larger than horsecars, but

SUNNYSIDE FROM THE HUDSON

This oil painting, by an unknown artist c. 1850, shows Irving's home, the tracks of the Hudson River Railroad.

GOUVERNEUR KEMBLE

It was Washington Irving's friend, Gouverneur Kemble, who convinced Irving to allow the railroad to cut across his land along the Hudson. The original of this photograph of Kemble is by Matthew Brady.

the important thing was the time consumed. From Chambers Street to Peekskill the running time was usually an hour and a half. Even the captains of the fastest steamboats shuddered at such competition. For $4,000 each, car manufacturers in Albany and Springfield, Massachusetts, were delivering coaches with mahogany seat backs, mahogany doors, walls paneled in satinwood, and plushly upholstered seats. Ceiling lights burned whale oil so that the fifty-two seated passengers could at least read the headlines of their evening papers. The young nation copied the European "caste" system of first- and second-class cars, the latter having no plush cushions, but hard varnished-wood seats instead.

From the days of the first sloops, the Highlands had always been a topographical bugaboo. The winds there had becalmed sloops or driven them on the rocks. The narrow channels and rocky outcroppings had worried steamboat captains. Now the mountains threatened the rail line, especially the way in which the towering cliffs rose up perpendicularly from the water. As far as Royers Hook, it was easy to follow the riverbank; above that the engineers' troubles began. For a while the surveyors toyed with the idea of turning inland to avoid steep places like Anthony's Nose, but this would have meant grades of more than ten or fifteen degrees and would have shattered all hope of a water-level route. Finally, the builders decided to tunnel through the Nose.

But the problems posed by influential men were perhaps even more troublesome than those presented by nature. One of these was General J. Watson Webb, who had a beautiful estate at Beekmantown. After the rails had been laid along the edge of his property on the riverbank, he charged that the railroad had promised, in return for the right-of-way, to stop any but the fastest through-express trains at his home for the convenience of himself, his wife, his family, and house guests. The railroad officials denied this, asking whether it was proper for its trains to have to stop whenever the general was in a mood for it. Webb attempted to get William B. Astor to support him, pointing out that the latter had objected to the railroad's cutting through his

Private Carriage. Carriage for Passengers. Car with Freight. Locomotive Engine.

RAILROAD, ENGINE, AND CARRIAGES.

Drawn by A. J. Davis, and engraved by A. J. Mason, for Williams's Register.

EARLY NEW YORK RAILROAD TRAIN

This illustration of an early New York railroad train, showing locomotive
freight and passenger carriages, was drawn by A. J. Davis (1803–1892) and
engraved by A. J. Mason (1794–?) for Williams's *New-York Annual Register*,
1832.

HUDSON RIVER RAILROAD TUNNEL AT ANTHONY'S NOSE

Railroad builders decided to tunnel through the steep slope at Anthony's Nose, rather than divert the line inland. This woodcut is from an 1853 issue of the *People's Journal*.

front lawn at Rhinebeck; but Astor was noncommittal and so the fuss finally died down.

Until the Hudson line was finished, travelers had to put up with minor annoyances at each end. In New York City the main station was at 32nd Street, where the engine roundtable was located. To get from the Chambers Street station to that depot, riders were carried in cars pulled by horses. Then the cars were taken over by the steam engines. At the upriver end of the line, steamboats met the trains at whatever point the rails had reached and from there carried the passengers on to Albany.

On October 1, 1851, for the first time, trains left New York and ran on the NY&HRR tracks all the way to Greenbush, the ferry station across from Albany, and back. Matthew Vassar in Poughkeepsie was very happy; so were hundreds of thousands of other persons in all walks of life. An article in the New York *Daily Times*, by a reporter who had made the inaugural run up the river, found the autumnal scenery breathtaking, the weather perfect, and the motion of the train so smooth that "even at forty miles an hour" reading was easy, and writing, for those who had to report the news, not too difficult. He thought the signal guards along the right-of-way were the perfect answer to those who expressed concern for their own safety. The four hours' ride, he said, was neither boring nor unpleasant, but it did generate 'a healthy appetite in the two hundred dignitaries who made the historic trip.

When they all sat down at table in a huge roundhouse cleaned and polished for the occasion, it must have been a striking sight. With a table set on each of the twenty repair tracks radiating from the central hub of the roundhouse, the scene resembled a giant wheel, each spoke covered with white linen and huge amounts of food. In the journalist's words, "All seated, the champagne artillery soon drowned the clatter of knife and fork, playing strange variations to the music of a band in attendance."

Four hours between the great port on the Atlantic and the capital city of Albany! What a blow to the steamboats! Businessmen turned from boat to train almost overnight; and before the first fiscal year was over the railroad had carried 765,877 passengers, although it had not been open all the way to Albany for more than a fourth of that time. What really vexed the steamboat interests were the fares charged by their land competitor. The fast expresses, which took less than four hours on the New York–Albany run after the initial kinks were removed, charged $2.50 per customer. They stopped at only five places en route: Hudson, Rhinebeck, Poughkeepsie, Fishkill, and Peekskill. For slightly slower express travel the charge was $2. Every evening a sort of patchwork train with mail cars, baggage cars, and coaches left Chambers Street in Manhattan for its upstate destination. It stopped at many stations along the line, taking on riders, mail, newspapers, freight, luggage, milk, and produce in season. To reach Albany required a whole night's travel and the riders had to sit up on wooden seats, but for braving these inconveniences all they had to pay was $1.25. A similar train operated in the reverse direction.

For many years mail trains ran on Sunday, but passenger trains did not. For a long time there were no railroad stations except in a few of the larger cities. Space was rented in buildings close to the track and agents were told to live near enough so that they could be of assistance, if needed, "twenty-four hours a day." In return they were paid the handsome salary of $30 a month.

In the decade before the Civil War and during that conflict, from about 1851 to 1865, the new railroad fought for its very life. Its passenger traffic was heavy—for those days—but it did not offset the expenses. Moreover, the expense of building the line, especially around and under the mountains at the river's edge, had been far costlier than anticipated. Operating costs, even in an age of modest salaries, were extremely high. The new railroad, although shorter in distance than most other lines, ran more trains than any competitor and ran them faster, owing to the water-level construction.

Corporate managers realized that if they meant to run a safe railroad they would need many things, particularly able-bodied men. So they positioned men at every drawbridge, road crossing, factory spur, tunnel, sharp curve, or trestle where the en-

AMERICAN EXPRESS TRAIN

By the 1850s, fast express trains ran regularly from New York to Albany along the Hudson. This classic lithograph of an American Express Train, published by Currier and Ives in 1864, shows a Hudson River steamboat in the background.

gineer could not see the track ahead. Each man had a wooden pole with a red flag on one end and a white flag on the other for daylight hours and red and white lanterns for darkness. In addition, each watchman was equipped with a spike maul and spikes, shovel, crowbar, and wrench, so that between trains they could help maintain the right-of-way. Among unsung heroes, these signalmen must surely stand high. Only one who has put in a twelve-hour stint in the open beside the Hudson when the mercury sometimes registers below zero and the winds blow off the river like bits of shattered glass can imagine what these watchmen endured. They could take some satisfaction, perhaps, in knowing that their railroad was the only one with a signal guard and that it operated at the fastest speeds in the land.

Curiously enough, the worst rail accident of those early days happened in a manner that showed that even the most careful precautions do not always protect. On a bitter February night in 1871, the Pacific Express was involved in a horrible wreck for which the signal guard on duty was in no way responsible. The train in question consisted of a baggage car, express car, five sleepers, and a day coach. A little after 10 P.M., David Simmons, the engineer, tooled his train on to the trestle over Wappinger's Creek at New Hamburgh. On the other track, southbound, a freight rolled on to the same trestle, derailed, and spilled its foremost cars all over the bridge. There was no time for a warning. The fireman jumped, but Simmons remained in the cab, trying to slow the train's speed. Among the derailed freight cars were tank cars filled with oil. The Pacific Express locomotive plowed into the jumble and ignited the oil before plunging into the creek below with baggage and express cars falling on top of it. Simmons died within seconds. Next behind the baggage car was the Buffalo sleeper, which stayed on the tracks but was engulfed by flames. Not one occupant came out alive. When the fire was extinguished the count showed twenty-two dead, five of them employees of the railroad. Within three seconds, in a distance of less than one hundred feet, everything had gone wrong.

Commodore Cornelius Vanderbilt, who had amassed a fortune with steamboats, now acquired all the railroads between

166

COMMODORE CORNELIUS VANDERBILT

Commodore Cornelius Vanderbilt (1794–1877), was responsible for the consolidation of twelve railroads between Albany and Buffalo into the New York Central Railroad. This portrait in oil on canvas is by Jared B. Flagg (1820–1899).

Albany and Buffalo—twelve in number—and renamed them the New York Central. Then, he gobbled up the Hudson River line by cleverly manipulating the market in its securities. It was alleged that the Commodore had "watered" the stock, but the courts exonerated him. In the end he controlled a rail line extending from Manhattan Island to Lake Erie at Buffalo. Later he created an even vaster complex, and his son William Henry extended the system—with a four-track roadbed—all the way to Chicago. By the 1880s and 1890s, the steamboats had given up their battle against the railroads, although a few continued to serve a limited need.

Commodore Vanderbilt was not the only financial magnate with vision in New York. Others felt that the Hudson-Mohawk break in the Appalachian barrier also justified a railroad. Early in 1881 these men began building the New York West Shore and Buffalo line from Weehawken in New Jersey north behind the Palisades to Haverstraw Bay and then along the western lip of the Hudson riverbank. Those who thought that the Hudson River line was an arduous feat of engineering now witnessed the even greater difficulties faced on the opposite shore. But by August 1883, the West Shore line was operating as far as Syracuse and building a roadbed on toward Buffalo.

Underneath the apparent success was the specter of bankruptcy. It was costing far too much money to build the road. Pay cuts were introduced, loans were made at high interest, and finally, after a bitter two-year war with its powerful rival on the opposite banks of the Hudson and Mohawk Rivers, the line was taken over by that rival. Now the wealthy New York Central held undisputed sway: for most of its length within New York State it had an unrivaled six-track roadbed.

Throughout the world the railroad was changing the life style of millions of human beings, matching speed with luxury. While the Hudson line did not have a funeral coach, like the one the Harlem line supplied for mourning parties riding from Manhattan to the cemetery at Woodlawn, it did possess the finest cars the Wagner Company and later the Pullman empire could manufacture. Photographs of the interiors of these coaches and sleepers show them to be lavishly luxurious, prime examples of "conspicuous consumption."

Jacques Offenbach, the composer, toured America in the 1870s and left a vivid record of his reaction to the railway line along the Hudson. Calling the Pullman cars a "precious institution," he compared them with those of the *Compagnie des Wagons-Lits et des Grands Express Européens*, and the latter came off second best. He summed up his "admiration for American railways. . .by saying that they are really—a cradle on wheels." The Pullman sleepers intrigued him even more than the chair cars and lounges. When the porters made up the berths and strung the green curtains in front of them, Offenbach was entranced by "the noise of boots falling on the floor, or the pleasant rustling sound which reveals the removing of a skirt."

The composer was ensconced in his own berth while the train hurtled through the night along the Hudson, his mind more than a little occupied with the movements of a curtain behind which he had seen a very pretty young woman retire. Later he awoke to hear footsteps in the corridor, peeked out, and saw a man go out onto the platform to enjoy a cigar. A short time later the man came back inside and went—not to his own section— but to the young lady's. There was a flutter of excitement, low, whispered words, and then the man retreated, mouthing excuses for his "mistake." It was a scene repeated more than once until the famous green curtains gave way to steel doors.

Foreign visitors, more than Americans, noticed how busy the Hudson was. This was not unusual. Native Americans, witnessing the many changes occurring as the nation became more and more industrialized, had come to take them for granted. But listen to Emile de Damseaux, a French traveler:

> This river, with its broad and deep waters, is covered throughout its length with every conceivable type of boat or vessel: we see huge gilt-encrusted ferries, several stories high, large wooden rafts; small canoes; enormous barges bulging with all kinds of merchandise and being pushed or pulled by powerful tugboats; gigantic ice boats of most

peculiar construction transporting a most precious and useful commodity to the sweltering masses of the great metropolis.

Commodore Vanderbilt wanted his passengers to have the best of everything and kept pace with rapid change. By the end of the nineteenth century the pattern was set for what was to follow. When the World's Columbian Exposition drew thousands to Chicago in 1893, the New York Central scheduled a twenty-hour train between that city and New York. It was called *The Exposition Flyer* and astounded travelers by both its speed and its luxury. Along with the *Empire State Express* and the *Lake Shore Limited*, the *Flyer* served to pave the way for still another de luxe train, one that was to be called "the greatest train in the world," the *Twentieth Century Limited*.

The *Twentieth Century Limited* was a fast, all-sleeper train with all the niceties and amenities the *haut monde* could wish for. Within the first month of its operation, it became the established leader among trains and retained its preeminence for more than half a century. For months Americans had been told, with much ballyhoo, that on June 15, 1902, a splendid new train would make the run between New York and Chicago while a sister train ran in the other direction. Handbills promised that the train would operate every day in the year and cover the 980 miles in twenty hours, and the New York Central proudly labeled it the fastest long-distance train in the world. The Central's arch-rival, the Pennsylvania Railroad, matched the *Century* with its *Twenty Hour Special*, but although the latter was well appointed and maintained a tight schedule, it never acquired the panache and renown of the *Twentieth Century Limited*.

A great train, the *Twentieth Century* tied the nation more tightly together, built fortunes, gave rise to legends of its own, and carried just about everyone who mattered. It fostered ballads and songs, and was the subject of a famous stage comedy and film. But, best of all, it stirred the hearts of countless men and women, boys and girls, who stood in awe as it sped by along the Hudson—until, as the wheel of progress turned, in the 1950s, it too sped into oblivion.

TWENTIETH CENTURY LIMITED
ON THE NEW YORK CENTRAL.

DINNER

BLUE POINTS

CONSOMME   PUREE OF TOMATOES

STUFFED MANGOES   CELERY   QUEEN OLIVES   CHOW CHOW
CALIFORNIA RIPE OLIVES   SALTED ALMONDS   PIN-MONEY PICKLES

BAKED REDSNAPPER
CUCUMBERS

BROILED FRESH MUSHROOMS ON TOAST
SWEETBREAD BRAISED WITH SPINACH   PEACH FRITTERS

RIBS OF PRIME BEEF   ROAST CHICKEN WITH DRESSING

MASHED POTATOES   BAKED SWEET POTATOES   ASPARAGUS
STRINGLESS BEANS IN CREAM   CORN

ROMAN PUNCH

ROAST TEAL DUCK

LETTUCE AND EGG SALAD   WATERCRESS SALAD

CHARLOTTE RUSSE
ENGLISH PLUM PUDDING, HARD AND BRANDY SAUCE
NEAPOLITAN ICE CREAM   ASSORTED CAKES   ORANGE MARMALADE
CALIFORNIA NAVEL ORANGES   APPLES   GRAPES   BANANAS
ROQUEFORT CHEESE   PHILADELPHIA N.Y. CREAM CHEESE
BENT'S CRACKERS
MOHAWK VALLEY MILK AND CREAM   COFFEE DEMI-TASSE   TEA

No charge for coffee demi-tasse served in Buffet Smoking or Observation Car.
Please procure check from dining car conductor.

MEALS, ONE DOLLAR

"LITHIA POLARIS"—PURE SPRING WATER FREE.
The drinking water served on the New York Central Dining Cars is from the celebrated "Polaris Springs" of the Boonville Mineral Spring Co., on the Rome, Watertown & Ogdensburg Division, in the foot-hills of the Adirondack Mountains. It has been analyzed by eminent chemists, and is absolutely pure.

A SOUVENIR MENU.
A copy of this Menu card in an envelope ready for mailing will be furnished free, on application, by the conductor in charge of this car.

The New-York Historical Society

DINING CAR MENU, *20th Century Limited*

The wide variety of items on the dinner menu for January 21, 1903, from the dining car of the *Twentieth Century Limited* reflects the luxurious class of accommodation for which the train was noted.

Chapter IX

Of Palaces and Pleasures

On one of her voyages up the Hudson, Harriet Martineau described a tiny white object perched atop a peak of the Catskills. When, upon inquiry she was told that it was the famous Catskill Mountain House, she announced determinedly that she would return and visit the hostelry. A seasoned world-traveler, she had heard of the place, which its owners called Pine Orchard House but an admiring world always referred to as the Mountain House. Built in 1823 in Greek Revival style, the edifice had lured the wealthy of both this country and Europe from the time of its opening. A few found fault with its architecture, and others, mostly of English background, curiously enough, did not think too highly of the cuisine. But not a single person failed to marvel at the hotel's breathtaking location as they gazed at the view from the front porch.

So when Harriet Martineau disembarked from a steamboat at Catskill on the afternoon of July 25, 1835, to visit the Mountain House, it had become a mecca for thousands who included it in an American "grand tour" that started in New York City, continued up the Hudson with stops at West Point and the Mountain House, and went on to include the springs at Saratoga and the beauty of Niagara Falls. Her ride over twelve miles of rough, rocky roads to the summit, 2,212 feet above the river, was hot and tiring, the horses' discomfort disturbed her sensitive nature, and she was aware of the parched fields lying under the

173

VILLAGE OF CATSKILL

Harriet Martineau might have encountered a scene such as this when she disembarked from a steamboat in July, 1835, on her way to the Catskill Mountain House. This lithograph of the village of Catskill by W. H. Bartlett (1809–1854), was published in London in 1839.

Sleepy Hollow Restorations

174

burning July sun. Then suddenly the stagecoach came out upon the grounds of the hotel and the myriad lights at the windows, turned on because of thunder clouds, conjured up the image of a fairy castle. That evening she sat on the piazza, watching lightning illuminate the hills and the distant ribbon below that was the Hudson. Rested by a good night's sleep, she arose the next morning, Sunday, to survey what seemed the whole world spread out before her.

Lyrically she wrote of the vista that emerged when the last of the morning mist was burned away. She exaggerated a bit, claiming to see not only the Green Mountains of Vermont, which are indeed visible on a clear day, but also the sparkle of the Atlantic Ocean far to the east. From her vantage point, the view was so dramatic she thought she detected in it something akin to the process of creation and was humbled by the sublime expanse of beauty that surrounded her.

Another admirer of the Catskill Mountain House was James Silk Buckingham, English author, editor, and founder of the London *Athenaeum* in 1828. On tour in this country, he became ill, and his physician ordered him to the resort in the mountains. He, too, like Harriet Martineau, rode the twelve arduous miles from the river landing to the hotel by stagecoach. This time, however, it rained while he was en route, torrents of water turning the road into a most dismal scene. At one point, hailstones battered the coach so hard the passengers thought they would all be thrown over the side into the forest below. When on the following day he beheld the enchanting vista from the piazza, he said it was worth traveling more than a hundred miles to see.

"The table, however, was, like all the American tables of hotels, steamboats, and boarding houses that we had yet seen more remarkable for the superabundance of food than skill or delicacy in preparing it," he wrote. Perhaps his temporary indisposition made him find fault with the terrapin soup, the canvasback and grouse, the sirloin steak and shad for which the Mountain House was famous, but of the view he rhapsodized:

. . .the full glory of a meridian sun beamed down upon one

175

CATSKILL MOUNTAIN HOUSE

From the river landing in the village of Catskill, a twelve mile stagecoach ride took visitors to the magnificent Catskill Mountain House, shown here in a lithograph by Currier and Ives.

of the most extensive and beautiful landscapes that could be well conceived. Behind us, to the westward, rose the peaks of mountains higher by a thousand feet and more, than the summit of that on which we stood, and completely intercepting all further view in that direction. To the east, however, the prospect was almost boundless.

In later years, at a halfway point on the road which climbed the hill, a small inn was built, ostensibly to supply refreshments for those wearied by the arduous drive from the river landing. It came to be known as the Rip Van Winkle House and was located on the very spot—according to local legend—where old Rip first encountered the little men who were playing at bowls.

Year after year the Catskill Mountain House lured the wealthy and famous to the crest of the mountains. Thomas Cole, the young artist who was mainly responsible for the birth of the Hudson River school of painting, went there in 1825, and his pictures of it attracted attention in the galleries of New York City. Other artists such as Asher Durand, Frederick Church, and George Inness followed in his footsteps and made the Mountain House one of the most easily recognized landmarks in all America. Washington Irving was enthusiastic about the place and Aaron Burr was a visitor in the early days. James Fenimore Cooper, Irving's literary rival, used the site in his novel *The Pioneers*. Cooper had one of his characters, Natty Bumppo, comment on the scene as it existed before the hotel was built, declaring that the view stretched for seventy miles. It actually does extend fifty miles up and down the Hudson, so the exaggeration was not so great.

Near the resort hotel were the Kaaterskill Falls (or Kaaterskill Clove), a natural wonder that appealed to artists and ordinary visitors alike. Irving described the gorge as "wild, lovely, and shagged, the bottom filled with fragments from the impending cliffs, and scarcely lighted by the reflected rays of the setting sun."With a drop longer than that of Niagara, though nowhere near the volume of water, the falls were considered a "must" by many tourists on their trips around the United States.

177

Engraved by J.C.Buttre.

and believe me, dear Sir,
as ever yours very sincerely

J. Fenimore Cooper

JAMES FENIMORE COOPER

The popular American author James Fenimore Cooper set many of his novels in the Hudson Valley. *The Pioneers* was set largely in the Catskills, and an earlier novel, *The Spy*, sub-titled "A Tale of the Neutral Ground," took place in Westchester County. This engraving of Cooper, including a facsimile of his signature, is by J. C. Buttre (1821–1893), based upon an 1850 Daguerreotype by Matthew Brady.

Of Palaces and Pleasures

After the Civil War the Catskill Mountain House took over much of the social *éclat* that had been enjoyed by Hot Springs in Virginia and White Sulphur Springs in West Virginia. After all, hadn't Jenny Lind given a concert there? Hadn't Oscar Wilde, that controversial writer from England, put on a skit there? And hadn't Alexander Graham Bell personally installed the first telephone in the building? So the personalities came. Ulysses S. Grant and William Tecumseh Sherman, fresh from the victories that had defeated the Confederacy and preserved the Union, hurried to the Catskills to loll upon the wide piazza. Later, President Chester A. Arthur stayed at the resort to get away from the cares of office in Washington and, presumably, the wretched muggy summer climate along the Potomac.

As the first resort in the Catskill Mountains, and possibly the first mountain resort in the United States, the hotel grew in fame and favor. It had accommodations for about five hundred guests, and most rooms had windows affording a splendid view of the Hudson Valley. There were rocking chairs on the piazza, although they do not seem to have been as popular then as the ones that later became a trademark of the hostelries at Saratoga Springs. People—except for the very old—wanted to see the surrounding sights as well. They rode in carriages to the valleys and lakes behind the hotel, hiked to the top of higher mountains behind the one on which the resort was built, or went with picnic baskets to dine *al fresco* among what Harriet Martineau called "the little nooks in the road, crowded with bilberries, cherries and alpine plants, and the quiet tarn, studded with golden water lilies."

Candlelight changed to gaslight and that in turn yielded to electric light. The stagecoach gave way to the train and then to the automobile. Airplanes intruded into the peace and quiet of the Catskills without doing too much harm since they seldom landed closer than Albany, and brought guests from far and near. Somehow the Mountain House absorbed all the shocks of change until the Great Depression of the 1930s. But thenceforth there was no recovery. In 1942, the hotel welcomed its last guests. After that, decay and neglect set in. In 1963, before air

179

KAATERSKILL FALLS

Washington Irving described the Kaaterskill Falls as "wild,
lovely, and shagged, the bottom filled with fragments from the
impending cliffs, and scarcely lighted by the reflected rays of the
setting sun." This steel engraving by W. H. Bartlett
(1809–1854), was published in *American Scenery*, c. 1840.

180

pollution had become such a momentous issue, the New York State Conservation Department, fearing injury to prowlers, burned the ruins down. The land, including Kaaterskill Falls, now belongs to the State.

The Catskill Mountain House was a mirror of its times, a lodestone for the prominent and the subject of innumerable passages in books and scenes on canvas and copperplate. Its epitaph, perhaps, is best expressed in the words of Harriet Martineau, who wrote of "this noblest wonder" of the Hudson Valley, "I would rather have missed the Hawk's Nest, the Prairies, the Mississippi, and even Niagara, than this."

With better means of transportation and a rising standard of living many upriver communities became resorts for New York City's denizens. Saratoga is an outstanding example of such development.

The first white man to see the springs at Saratoga was the French Jesuit missionary-martyr, Isaac Jogues, in 1643. Over a century later, the British colonial official, Sir William Johnson, appointed Superintendent of Indian Affairs because of his successful dealings with the Indians of the Six Nations, visited Saratoga several times. According to one account, he was carried by faithful Indians to what was then called High Rock Spring after he was wounded in 1755 at the Battle of Lake George. They nursed him tenderly and restored him to health. Another version says that Sir William, known as "Johnson of the Mohawks," was always attended by a covey of pretty Indian women, for whom he showed even-handed affection, playing few favorites. He himself admitted to fathering a hundred children by these women, so it may have been out of a feeling of deep respect and awe that the Mohawks took him to their secret spa.

The Indians were sure that Manitou, the Great Spirit, had created the medicinal springs near the Upper Hudson just for their own welfare. The white men who moved into the upper reaches of New York while it was still a colony took over the belief with the land. Since then, the waters have been sought for their curative value by rich and poor, natives and foreigners, presidents, generals, tycoons, and the social élite as well as by the general public. For almost 150 years, Saratoga has been a vacation center for "society, sport, and sin," as John Reed aptly phrased it.

Rumors and early tall tales aside, Saratoga leaped into prominence ahead of Virginia's Warm Springs and Connecticut's Stafford Springs when Gideon Putnam put up the first big hotel in 1800 and set about promoting the medicinal benefits to be derived from drinking the foul-tasting effluents that poured from three separate orifices in the earth. Putnam was a far-sighted businessman who looked upon Saratoga as a promising investment. George Washington himself had entertained the idea of buying the Springs.

In early America, when ailments failed to respond to medical treatment, many looked toward Saratoga as their best hope. If one had yellow jaundice, or suffered from habitual constipation, scrofula, dyspepsia, and other diseases or dysfunctions, its promoters suggested that persistent ingestion of the waters at Saratoga would bring relief.

Martin Van Buren, the "fox of Kinderhook," President of the United States, 1837–1841, was clever enough to make Saratoga *his* resort, knowing that his regular presence there during the season would be highly beneficial to New York, his home state. Raised on the Hudson in Columbia County, he had a warm spot in his heart for anything connected with the river. Saratoga was, of course, a few miles in from the west bank but it was close enough to the historic Saratoga battlefield, bounded on one side by the river, to win his approval. By the time Van Buren was helping to set the social tone at the Springs, there were several prestigious hotels in Saratoga, the largest being Putnam's Union Hall, Congress Hall, the Pavilion, and the United States Hotel.

The Springs appealed to people widely for assorted reasons. One of the earliest celebrities to visit the resort was Madame Jumel, who had exploited an exceptionally pretty figure and keen mind to achieve wealth and notoriety. She consorted with various men in an effort to gain social acceptance, even wedding

SARATOGA SPRINGS

During the early 1800s, Saratoga Springs became an extremely popular resort, and has remained so to this day. This illustration is from Milbert's *Picturesque Itinerary of the Hudson River.*

Aaron Burr when he was on the very edge of the grave. She summered at the United States Hotel, clad in Paris finery, surrounded by servants, waited upon by lackeys, and carted around in a gaudy carriage. Yet, she was almost totally ignored by the society-minded female guests, although it must have been a difficult feat indeed to ignore such a striking figure in a canary-yellow carriage with two liveried men sitting on the box.

The virtuous and the not-so-virtuous lived in surprising harmony at the Springs. Perhaps the former were too busy drinking the waters and eating to be aware of the seamier aspects of the town. It must have been a peculiar existence for the "good" people: they ate three meals a day that would have taxed a Canadian lumberjack and did little else but sit and gossip. This, of course, was before the racetrack came. Buckingham said the people ate as if the world were coming to an end.

A foreigner, he was also an excellent observer, eminently fair and as willing to praise as to blame. Asserting that nowhere in the whole world of fashionable society resorts were there so many beautiful women as at Saratoga, Buckingham waxed almost lyrical in his descriptions of their pure complexions, their alabaster flesh tones, and the amplitude of their figures. But on the subject of love and passion, he gave them poor marks:

> They have no passion at all. I have neither heard nor seen any evidence of an all-absorbing and romantic feeling in them; although probably the American women make the most faithful of wives, I do not think they love with the same intensity as the women of Europe.

Saratoga was for the most part a summer refuge for decent ordinary people, with a sprinkling of the famous and the infamous, at least until the Civil War. It was "the waters" that lured people from their homes. Southern aristocrats liked the northern spa and so did Washingtonians, thankful for any excuse to get out of the Potomac swamplands. Change—drastic change—came to the Springs in the penultimate year of the Civil War. In 1864 a racetrack was opened there, and thenceforth the curative

MADAME ELIZA JUMEL (MRS. AARON BURR)

This portrait of Madame Eliza Jumel, after she married Aaron Burr, is from an undated lithograph published in Paris.

waters from the Springs were almost forgotten.

The Southern aristocrats who frequented Saratoga before the war had enjoyed racing. They had subsidized a place of their own called the Oklahoma Track and wagered small sums on the races. But there was an aloofness, a sense of exclusivity, about their venture: the common man, especially the Northerner, was not made to feel welcome. When they took their thoroughbreds away after the outbreak of hostilities, there was a void to be filled. Northerners like William R. Travers, John Hunter, and Leonard Jerome—the maternal grandfather of Winston Churchill—were not slow to see this. Racing made August *the* month in Saratoga. Overnight, it didn't matter which foul-tasting water you downed, so long as you picked a winner at the track. You rose early, went to the "old Oklahoma" for the exercising of the horses, and then to breakfast before walking across the road to the new track to watch the running. With the fast horses came also the gamblers, touts, "con" men, and fast women. The owners called themselves "The Saratoga Association for the Improvement of the Breed of Horses."

"Boss" William M. Tweed and later Richard Croker—political bosses of Manhattan—visited Saratoga to hold some councils of war away from overinquisitive reform groups. Commodore William Vanderbilt and his son, William K., also liked the Springs. "Diamond Jim" Brady, a steady customer, was cherished by the porters, waiters, and barkeeps who knew he was an extravagant tipper. With him came Lillian Russell, that Valkyrian sex goddess of the era.

President Ulysses S. Grant liked the spa and was a well-known figure in the Grand Union's barroom, with its polished mahogany bar almost as long as the piazza in front of the hotel. George Law, head of the Eighth Avenue Street Car line in New York, gave jewels to various ladies there with casual abandon; and Jimmy Hilton, whose father owned the Grand Union at the time, spent more than $20,000 on precious stones for a reigning musichall favorite, Della Fox, who burst upon the scene like a comet and disappeared almost as quickly—a victim of acute alcoholism.

RACETRACK AT SARATOGA SPRINGS

Originally published in the August 14, 1875, edition of *Frank Leslie's Illustrated Newspaper*, these sketches show "jockeys exercising their horses in front of the grand stand previous to the race," and "a start for a mile-and-three-quarter dash" on the racetrack at Saratoga Springs.

WILLIAM MARCY ("BOSS") TWEED

William Marcy Tweed (1823–1878), popularly known as "Boss" Tweed, served as a New York State Senator, United States Congressman, and political leader of New York's Tammany Hall organization.

LILLIAN RUSSELL

Lillian Russell (1861–1922), who later became the virtual Queen of Saratoga, as photographed before she attained national prominence c. 1878 by Jose Mora.

Of Palaces and Pleasures

Lillian Russell was the real queen of Saratoga, becoming a fixture there, along with Diamond Jim Brady and Jesse Lewisohn, another of her devoted admirers. Brady gave her a carriage trimmed in silver which she drove about the spa's elm-shaded streets, using white doeskin reins. Later she toured the resort in 1904–model motorcars, which, instead of leather upholstery, had seat coverings of gaudy chintz. Miss Russell always stayed in one of the many cottages maintained by the hotels, attended by a flock of young and pretty girls whom she called her "Farm Flirts," and whose evenings were devoted to entertaining gentleman friends. They were more fortunate than their chaperone (an odd name indeed!) when it came time to go to dinner. The story circulated that the buxom Miss Russell's efforts to squeeze into her corset involved at least two maids and that the tug of war consumed up to thirty minutes before the strings were tied. For, at the turn of the century, American tastes in feminine pulchritude were quite different from current preferences. Clarence Day perhaps best summed up the masculine feeling about Miss Russell in three sentences: "There was plenty of her to see, and we liked that. We liked flesh. Her hips were so gorgeous and stately, her broad white bosom so ample."

Those who attended the races saw others besides this goddess figure: Edna Wallace Hopper, Edna May, and a host of young society belles. And, of course, Anna Held, the actress wife of Florenz Ziegfeld, who caused a stir by attributing her peaches-and-cream complexion to daily baths in a tub filled with milk. On a less theatrical level, individuals like Jim Fisk, Jay Gould, Bernard Baruch, Jock Whitney, Samuel Riddle, and Big Jim Morrissey lent their names and fame to the spa in many ways. Big Jim, for example, brought organized gambling to Saratoga.

As the old Oklahoma race course had antedated major racing there, so had other gambling houses preceded Morrissey's Club-House. A former prizefighter of gargantuan proportions, Morrissey was also a bigwig of Tammany Hall, and served two terms as a representative in Congress. He had a gambling casino in New York City, and Saratoga seemed a likely place to expand

MORRISSEY'S GAMBLING HOUSE AT SARATOGA SPRINGS

Women and permanent residents of the town of Saratoga Springs were denied entrance to Big Jim Morrissey's Club-House, shown here in an illustration from the September 9 , 1871, edition of *Every Saturday*.

his operations. Overcoming some resistance by judicious gifts and bribes and promises to run a "clean" place, he won approval, and built the Club-House, vowing never to allow a woman or a permanent resident of Saratoga Springs to enter the building. But his promise was not long-lived, for he died at the age of forty-seven.

But not until Richard A. Canfield entered upon the scene did Saratoga know the meaning of big stakes at the gaming tables. One of the first things he did after getting control of the Saratoga Club-House was to enlarge and beautify the grounds. Canfield continued Morrissey's edict banning women from the gaming rooms, but he permitted them to dine in his restaurant, an establishment of rare epicurean delight. Its chef, Jean Columbin, was paid $5,000 for a two-month season and given a handsome expense account to spend the other ten months roaming Europe to acquire ideas for new and succulent dishes. Canfield was not concerned that the restaurant lost large sums of money consistently; the eating establishment was a magnet to attract people to the gaming tables.

Many vivid little details remain associated with Saratoga. An angry cook, upbraided because his French-fried potatoes were too large, shaved another potato into thin slices, deep-fried them, and became famous as inventor of the Saratoga Chip. Just as memorable was the main piece of luggage then in vogue, a huge trunk with a lid humped to prevent piling one on top of another, quite naturally called the Saratoga trunk. People also recalled the night on which Berry Wall was put off the dance floor at the Grand Union for wearing a black-tie dinner jacket tailored by the dean of men's tailors, Henry Poole. At the Grand Union it was full dress with white tie or nothing.

But of all the memories, surely the most vivid must be that of the night when John "Bet-a-Million" Gates lost $150,000 at the faro table before dinner, asked that the stakes be raised to $5,000 and $10,000, made good his loss before midnight, and went on to win $250,000 by dawn.

In his upstairs office, Dick Canfield had a safe with five combinations and three steel doors. Inside those three doors he kept a million dollars in cash, proof that the play at the Club-House was bigger than that at the largest casinos in Europe. But eventually the racetrack started taking the spotlight away from the gambling casino. Backed by William C. Whitney and supported by such socialites as Cornelius Vanderbilt, Ogden Goelet, and Caroline Astor, the track lured the cream of society back to Saratoga. Extremely wealthy, they felt no urge to gamble, but took their stables with them to the Springs as today's traveler takes his camper. They restored the old stake races—the Alabama, Travers, and Spinaway—and after decades of success even restored the medicinal springs themselves.

One morning during the height of the 1907 season, the racing crowds saw a new sign: "For sale—this entire block." Canfield was selling the casino and all its appurtenances. No one seemed to want the property, and it remained vacant for years until the town of Saratoga bought it for a museum. In the years that followed there were other casinos, flamboyant, lavishly furnished, but they did not long endure.

After World War I, notorious gangsters entered the field. Arnold Rothstein ran the Brook before he was cut down in a New York hotel suite and Charles "Lucky" Luciano operated the Chicago Club before being sent to jail. None of these gambling places had "class." Canfield's always did. Seven years after the "For Sale" notice went up on the grass in Saratoga, the gambler had a fatal fall down the stairs of the subway station at 14th Street in New York City—and now is best remembered for the game of solitaire that bears his name.

"Old Smoke," as Big Jim Morrissey was often called, made money in any way he could. It flowed into his coffers from his gambling casino, from politics, and from horse racing. Living each summer in Saratoga, he was bound to see moneymaking possibilities in Saratoga Lake; hence it was logical for him to entice boating clubs from the larger eastern cities to race there. When college crews followed, no one was surprised.

The first intercollegiate regatta on Lake Saratoga was held in 1874, bringing together the slim shells of Yale, Harvard, Columbia, Cornell, Dartmouth, and Princeton. In those days six men constituted a college crew. Columbia, having been taught what was called the English stroke, won handily. That race initiated intercollegiate rowing. The next year college crews swarmed into Saratoga. It was a fortunate thing that the lake was wide, for when the starting gun sounded there were boats from Bowdoin, Union, Brown, Williams, Cornell, Harvard, Princeton, Amherst, Hamilton, Wesleyan, Columbia, Dartmouth, and Yale. From all over the East crowds traveled to the lake, until some thirty thousand spectators were assembled. Cornell won that race, nosing out Columbia by a whisker. Another race was held the next year, but then Saratoga lost favor as the shells grew to eight-oared boats with coxswains to set the stroke and steer the craft. The regattas moved to Lake George, Cayuga Lake, the Delaware River, the Thames, and the Connecticut. Twice more, in 1884, and again 1898, the collegians returned to Lake Saratoga, but after that they were gone forever.

For Hudson River residents this was a stroke of good fortune. After trying out various bodies of water, the college crews picked the Hudson at Poughkeepsie for their big yearly regatta and soon this became the big rowing event in the United States. Like so many national institutions, the Poughkeepsie regatta was not born without travail and pain. Just above the town of Poughkeepsie the Hudson straightens out into what the Dutch pioneers had called De Lange Rak, the long reach, and for four miles it is a virtual straightaway. Officials from Columbia, Cornell, and Pennsylvania decided that this was the ideal spot, and in 1895 held their first race there.

Just as the first regatta at Saratoga had lured thousands, so did the opening race of the mid-Hudson classic. Weeks before the day of the contest, aficionados of the sport rented rooms at the Nelson House and other hotels and boardinghouses until every room in town was taken. Carpenters and ironworkers from the roundhouses and yards of the West Shore Railroad labored across the river in Highland, turning a long string of flat cars into a rolling grandstand, with tiered benches facing the river.

On Friday, June 21, thousands of enthusiasts rode the ferry over to the far shore, where some climbed aboard the observa-

The excitement of a college regatta is captured in this woodcut by A. B. Frost (1851–1928), from *Harper's Weekly*, July 17, 1883.

195

tion train and others crowded the riverbank. As the train waited, engine huffing and puffing, and the crews put their shells in the water, a tugboat carrying Governor Levi P. Morton of New York came upriver. The captain ignored orders that powered craft avoid the area. When the tug reached the float where the Pennsylvania shell was tied up, it rammed the racing vessel and broke it in half. More than one Pennsylvania citizen swore he would never vote for Levi Morton for President, even when the Governor said he would pay for a replacement. Experts from the boatyards started hurriedly to repair the shell and the race was postponed until Monday.

On that day the water was choppy. The Pennsylvania crew, deciding to try for an early lead, set out rowing like mad. For a mile they did well, but then the patched-up shell started to ship water. The rival crews passed Pennsylvania near the railroad bridge, and when they came out from under the arches the damaged boat broke in two. Columbia won handily. That night is one Poughkeepsie may never forget. The roistering lasted until dawn. Sheriffs waved their guns in a vain attempt to restore order; the saloons ran out of beer by midnight and hard liquor by 2 A.M. When frenzied Columbia supporters shot skyrockets along the bar in the Nelson House the proprietors abruptly shut up shop. From that night on, the bar always closed on the day of the regatta.

Each year thereafter, except for the one at Saratoga Lake, the college crews raced on the Hudson. They built bigger and fancier boathouses on both shores, and undergraduates proved their college loyalty by painting huge letters on rocks and the faces of cliffs. Harvard rowed at Pougheepsie for one year only, then hied itself back to the Thames to race with Yale. Georgetown, Leland Stanford, and Massachusetts Institute of Technology showed up occasionally, but the regulars were Cornell, Columbia, Pennsylvania, Syracuse, and Navy at the beginning, joined later by big crews from Wisconsin, California, and Washington.

In 1929, the year of the Wall Street stock market crash, the intercollegiate regatta bore all the signs of a sea battle fought in a

Columbia University

197

VICTORIOUS 1929 COLUMBIA REGATTA CREW

The rugged 1929 intercollegiate regatta, plagued by rainstorms and high winds, was won by Columbia, whose victorious crew is shown in the photograph on page 197.

storm. The varsity race—scheduled after the freshman and junior varsity events—started late in the evening, with rain sheeting down and wind whipping the river's surface into a froth. To make matters worse, the shells had to face a strong headwind. Judges and stewards discussed postponing the event but the college men wanted to race; finally, just as darkness crept down into the valley, the eight-oared craft broke away from the starting line.

Almost at once they began shipping water. The boat from Massachusetts Institute of Technology was the first to go under. The rowers were picked up by their college launch and a line fastened to the shell, far below the surface. Then California, Cornell, and Syracuse found the rough water too much for them and their shells sank. Navy and Pennsylvania had heavy going and fell back, but they stayed afloat. The real contest was between Columbia and Washington. The crew from the Pacific Coast tried manfully, but Columbia that day was blessed not only with great power but astonishing "seamanship." The light blue shell took on water, but not enough to stop the burly rowers, and Columbia ended the four-mile contest well in the lead.

June was an exciting month in Poughkeepsie. Colleges around the country were no longer in session and the rowing crews training for the regatta were settled in on the river bank. To the girls at Vassar College, it was an especially exciting time. Matthew Vassar, the wealthy brewer who had helped get the railroad to run through town and founded the college for women in 1861, would undoubtedly have enjoyed Regatta Week. During the fifty-five years that the intercollegiate regatta was held at Poughkeepsie, it might even have brought smiles to the faces of "Trade" and "Mark" Smith, the brothers who manufactured cough drops in a basement using nothing but a stove, kettles, and their own two hands in 1850, and saw the business grow into a huge success.

Chapter X

Dreamers, Doers, Shakers, and Others

As the United States grew and expanded, the Hudson Valley did not cease to attract the doers. It also attracted the dreamers. From the earliest years of the Republic, men and women— dreaming of a better world or a millennial kingdom on earth— were drawn to the magnificent rich shores of the Hudson. The earliest such efforts were motivated by religion. In the late eighteenth century Ann Lee— "Mother Lee"— set up a colony of Shakers ("Shaking Quakers") in Watervliet, near Albany. She traveled widely in that area, attempting to set up other colonies of her sect, the official name of which was "United Believers in Christ's Second Appearing." One such offshoot, in New Lebanon, west of Pittsfield, Massachusetts, proved far more enduring than the others. Its members were excellent farmers and artisans, experimenting successfully with seeds and herbs, weaving textiles proficiently, and making sturdy furniture and farm implements.

To the north of the Shaker communes, in Washington County, William Miller and his Millerites established their religious colony and awaited the imminent end of the world. Despite their neighbors' ridicule and disbelief, the Millerites stubbornly clung to their fundamentalist beliefs and by 1845 numbered some fifty thousand Adventists, as they came to be called. They are

SHAKER SETTLEMENT AT WATERVLIET, NEW YORK

A 1941 photograph of buildings in the Shaker colony established by Mother Ann Lee in the late 18th century in Watervliet, near Albany.

still active and numerous as a religious sect, 130 years after William Miller awaited the Day of Last Judgment in his commune near Hudson Falls.

Others among the colonies established in the Hudson Valley in those first decades of the nineteenth century were utopian socialist in character, influenced by the communes set up in France by the social reformers Fourier and Cabet. Robert Owen, the son of a Welsh saddlemaker, who himself became a prosperous cotton-textile manufacturer at New Lanark, Scotland, founded several communal colonies in the United States—one at Haverstraw in 1825 and a later one at Coxsackie. The Owenites' communes were based on rationalism and strongly imbued with early socialist and cooperative principles. Openly at odds with the established churches and religions, they aroused much opposition from the residents of the surrounding Rockland County communities. Owen himself, a self-made man with social vision and idealism, spent much of his substantial fortune on these experiments in social living. Unfortunately, they suffered not only from the pressures and hostility of the outside world, but were also "betrayed by what is false within": individual dissensions, power struggles, impracticality, and lofty ideals too much ahead of their time. Owen's best-known commune was at New Harmony, Indiana (1825); but it is worth mentioning his lesser-known and equally ill-fated efforts here on the shores of the Hudson—in this instance "a river of lost dreams," to use Carl Carmer's phrase.

Perhaps the least known but certainly one of the most compelling attempts to build a commune was undertaken by a handful of New York City Jews in 1838. Near Kingston, in the Ulster County village of Wawarsing, this tiny group bought five hundred acres of land on a sparse plateau of the Shawangunk Mountains as a haven of refuge for Jewish people—a new Jerusalem. They called it *Shalom* (Peace). They had a precedent, albeit an unhappy one: Major Mordecai Noah, an American Jewish writer, playwright, politician, and diplomat, had tried to set up a Jewish colony named Ararat on Grand Island near Niagara Falls in 1825. It was an abortive failure. The Shalom colony was also a dream that failed—yet in its four years of existence it proved to be sturdier and more motivated than most outsiders had thought possible.

A river as majestic as the Hudson, that inspired the creation of such new settlements, was bound also to motivate men of letters to describe its beauty and artists to capture its moods with oil, watercolor, and etching tool. The writers, beginning with Washington Irving, included James Fenimore Cooper, William Cullen Bryant, James Kirke Paulding, John Burroughs, Edith Wharton, Maxwell Anderson, and Carl Carmer, to name only a few. Some of the artists interested in the Hudson created their greatest works in a span of years that barely covered a half century. Yet, in that relatively short period (1825–1875) they achieved such distinction and popular acclaim that their work is referred to as the "Hudson River school."

Their work coincided with the young nation's beginning to gain self-assurance after two wars with the former mother-country. Pride in America's valor on the battlefield went hand in hand with deep esteem for commercial, scientific, and political progress. It was only natural for the upsurge of national self-respect to burgeon into cultural fields. Men and women now had a chance to see the beauty of America with leisure to enjoy it. Americans who boasted that they had twice defeated the then strongest world power could also vaunt their country's scenic charms. Niagara Falls may have been the most dramatic example; but the Hudson, with its changing vistas, moods, and colors, easily rivaled the Rhine or Danube.

The Hudson River school did not spring, phoenix-like, from the ashes of an earlier group of landscape artists. Its members learned their trade in many ways and places, in engraving plants, in studios in Paris and Rome, and in self-taught sessions where innate genius was the only available teacher. What brought the members of the "school" together was neither a single leader nor a universal point of view; it was the Hudson itself that nurtured these artists. Other American painters had preceded them, portrait artists like Gilbert Stuart, and masters of the seascape like Washington Allston. The artists of the Hudson River school devoted themselves to capturing the scenes along the river with what was almost photographic accuracy. For

203

WASHINGTON IRVING AND HIS LITERARY FRIENDS

"Washington Irving and his Literary Friends at Sunnyside," an oil painting by Christian Schussele (1824 or 1826–1879), depicts an imaginary gathering in Irving's study including such contemporaries as Oliver Wendell Holmes, Nathaniel Hawthorne, Henry Wadsworth Longfellow, James Kirke Paulding, Ralph Waldo Emerson, William Cullen Bryant, and James Fenimore Cooper.

the most part, the paintings they executed were realistic and understandable, eliciting approval from ordinary viewers and artists.

It is idle to speculate on which artist first established his claim to leadership in the Hudson River school. That honor is generally accorded to Thomas Cole, but Thomas Doughty, self-taught, preceded Cole with paintings that elicited some praise for their American genuineness. Cole is accepted as the first in his group because Doughty's scenes were somewhat idealized. His rivers could be any river. Cole's Hudson was *the* Hudson; there could be no mistake about it.

Cole, English-born, was trained in engraving and in designing patterns for the cloth manufactured by the cotton mills of the Midlands. Moving to this country as a young man in 1819, he traveled for a short distance up the Hudson and quickly convinced himself that he should concentrate on landscapes. By the time he was twenty-five, he had painted perhaps a half-dozen scenes which he sold almost as soon as he exhibited them in the window of a shop owned by a friend. The purchaser urged Cole to take a vacation in the Catskills—he had been working long hours to help support his father's family—and from this stay in the mountains came more paintings, and quick acceptance as a first-rate artist. Cole was a many-faceted individual who managed to write poetry, prose, and philosophical articles while sketching and painting. One of his descriptions of sunrise in the Catskills clearly illustrates the lure the Hudson held for him:

The mists were resting on the vale of the Hudson like drifted snow: tops of distant mountains in the east were visible—things of another world. The sun rose from bars of pearly hue: above there were clouds light and warm, and the clear sky was of a cool grayish tint. The mist below the mountains began first to be lighted up, and the trees on the tops of the lower hills cast their shadows over the misty surface—innumerable streaks. A line of light on the extreme horizon was very beautiful. Seen through the breaking mists, the fields were exquisitely fresh and green.

THOMAS COLE

Self-portrait in oil on canvas by Thomas Cole (1801–1848), who is generally considered the leader of the Hudson River School of painting.

Though dark, the mountainside was sparkling; and the Hudson, where it was uncovered to the sight, slept in deep shadow.

Philip Hone, urbane man of affairs and Mayor of New York, spotted Cole's talent and bought some of his earliest paintings. By 1828, the artist had assured himself a place of distinction as the foremost interpreter of the Hudson with brush and canvas. His success led others to emulate his work and in the rush of painters to the region, the Hudson River school was born. Cole's pictures of the Hudson were what showed him at his best. He was compulsively driven to put down the colors and shadings and details he saw in the glens and mountains of the Catskills, the placid coves of the Hudson, and the broad valleys where the river widened after its course through the Highlands.

Asher Durand, a friend of Cole's, was another of the pioneer artists who never wearied of the Hudson. A disciplined perfectionist, he too believed that art was tied closely to the interpretation of nature. He had been a well-known engraver before turning to landscapes. In fact, many other members of the Hudson River school started as engravers, John Casilear and John Frederick Kensett among them.

Most of these artists, and those who followed them, were young and all were friends. They all influenced one another, yet without indulging in mindless imitation or copying. Frederick E. Church, who studied under Cole for two years in the mountains, picked up some of his teacher's techniques but used them in such a different way that his finished landscapes were distinctly his own. Church may have profited financially more than any other in the group. His large paintings, virtual murals, appealed to a nation that swelled with pride in its wealth of scenery.

One after another, new artists rose to fame. Jasper Cropsey, Albert Bierstadt, George Inness, and David Johnson, among many, felt the lure of the Hudson River. No area of the river escaped attention: paintings of the lower harbor and the Jersey shore from Manhattan led inescapably to other views of the

207

ASHER B. DURAND

A friend of Thomas Cole, Asher B. Durand (1796–1886), was a well-known engraver as well as one of the pioneer artists of the Hudson River School. The artist of this illustration of Durand at work is unknown.

Palisades, Tappan Zee, Haverstraw Bay, the Highlands, the Catskills, and the calmer, more level terrain to the north.

Not all of these painters and others ostensibly belonging to the school limited their output to scenes of the Hudson. Church reached for greater heights with views of Niagara Falls and the high Andes; Bierstadt rode west with early military units to capture on canvas the rugged peaks of the Rockies. Yet their deep-rooted affection for the Hudson was demonstrated by the fact that some built their studios on its banks. Most of these studios were like traditional artists' workshops—simple shacks, renovated barns, or ordinary houses with windows letting in the northern light. Church, however, was not content with such a simple abode. Having traveled to Peru, Jamaica, Jerusalem, Damascus, Greece, Turkey, and Persia, he developed a passion for the exotic sights he had seen in those distant lands. A wealthy man, he built a home called Olana on the east bank of the Hudson across from Catskill. Olana was designed by Church with technical help from the architect Calvert Vaux. It was more a castle than a home. Done in locally quarried stone, Olana borrowed from both Moorish and Turkish styles, with Persian overtones, but instead of the usual Moorish inner court, it had a cruciform central hall off which opened an art gallery and living rooms.

From the 1820s to the 1870s, the landscapes of the Hudson River school of painting were known throughout America. Men and women who had never been out of the city at the mouth of the river felt that they knew every twist and turn in its channel, every cove, landing, hillside, and town along its course because of their familiarity with these paintings. There was a sense of reality about these works. The steamboat *America*, painted by James Bard, was like a naval architect's drawing, precise and detailed. Cropsey's shad fishermen were human beings, wet and grimy, tired from hauling in their nets; and the storm brewing over Storm King Mountain in Samuel Colman's painting is frightening in its authenticity. One expects lightning to come flaring out of the leaden blue skies at any moment as the fishermen hurry to get their little boats ready for the inevitable squall.

209

The Storm King on the Hudson, BY SAMUEL COLMAN

A storm is brewing over Storm King Mountain in this 1866 oil painting by Samuel Colman (1832–1920).

National Collection of Fine Arts, The Smithsonian Institution

What happened, then, to end the popularity of this group of landscape artists? Art historians and critics are unable to agree. George Inness, who had found Cole's and Durand's work so satisfying in his youth, broke away from tight adherence to their school. He wondered whether accuracy alone was enough, and strove to inject more of his own feelings into what he painted. Moreover, a new source of graphic exposition had arisen in the United States. Lithography, seized upon by Nathaniel Currier and James Merritt Ives, reproduced scenes by the thousands. Once they worked out the difficulties of mass production, no home in America was complete without at least one colorful rendition of the Chicago Fire, Home for Thanksgiving, Central Park, the Lightning Express Trains, or any one of several hundred other picture subjects. Artists like George Durrie and Fanny Palmer, although no match for Cole or Durand or Church, still had a knack for detail. To many viewers this was more than enough. Besides, small prints cost only fifteen and twenty-five cents, and the larger folios could be bought for a dollar or two. And, finally, there was the rise and growing popularity of photography.

By the 1880s, the Hudson River school was fading away, as if a mist from the river had moved quietly down upon it. But it was a native force that had given American painting a place in the world it could be proud of. Now that nearly a century has passed, people are once more turning admiringly to its works to see what life was like on the Hudson before industrial civilization trampled it with indelible footprints.

History devotes many of its pages to the famous, the wealthy, and the talented, but reserves few lines for the "mute inglorious" many. Yet, life along the river owed much to those whose names are no longer often spoken and who in their own ways contributed to the annals of the Hudson. There is, for instance, the story of one of the most unusual individuals to fight in the Revolutionary War, running into the time after the final curtain had fallen at Yorktown and truly stranger than fiction.

It begins in Middleboro, Massachusetts, where Deborah

GEORGE INNESS

Initially a follower of Thomas Cole and Asher Durand, George Inness (1825–1894) later broke away from the Hudson River School. This self-portrait is in oil on wood panel, 1872.

Sampson, growing up after her father's disappearance at sea, wearied of playing the dull menial role of an indentured house servant. Early in 1782, she walked out of her master's home, donned a man's clothes, and signed up as a private in the Continental Army, using the assumed name of Timothy Thayer. No one learned the truth about her until one evening, spending her bonus money in a local tavern, she became tipsy from unaccustomed drinking and was exposed.

Her church "withdrew fellowship," which was as close as a Protestant church could come to excommunicating her, and she was warned that the gates of Hell were yawning. But Deborah, though plain of visage, was stout-hearted and determined. With $12 she had saved from her pay, she bought material and secretly sewed together a man's suit of linsey-woolsey, then hiked seventy-five miles to Worcester, where she enlisted again, this time as Private Robert Shurtleff. Almost at once she was assigned to Captain George Webb's company, in the 4th Massachusetts Regiment of Foot.

Transferred to West Point, the company marched across the Berkshires to the Hudson with Private Shurtleff striding along unnoticed. Her brothers-at-arms wondered a little about the lack of whiskers on her face but there were many young boys in the company, so they paid scant attention. She was neither homely nor attractive, and she had tightly bound linen bandages around her chest to conceal her bosom. Soon the company was ordered into the Neutral Ground to halt Tory pilfering. Deborah and her fellow fighters marched down to the edge of New York, then retraced their steps until they reached Tappan Bay, between Tarrytown and Ossining. There they encountered a band of armed Tories. In the ensuing melee, Deborah behaved splendidly, fighting hand-to-hand until a saber blow floored her with a cut across the forehead. Back in camp at West Point she recovered, proud of her scar, and took time to write her mother that she had found "agreeable work" in "a large, but well-regulated family."

A few weeks later, in another guerrilla action, in East Chester, Private Shurtleff escaped an ambush with her fellows but received a bullet in her thigh. Knowing that she would be exposed by the field surgeon, she waited until his attention was attracted elsewhere and limped off into the woods. For days, she hid out, washing and dressing the wound until, because of her good health and youth, it healed. Sent north to Ticonderoga, the 4th Massachusetts found itself engaged with a band of Indians. Deborah got the upper hand with a warrior and was about to kill him when she realized he was a white captive. Instead she helped him back to camp. That was the end of her career along the Hudson.

She was next heard from in Philadelphia where she was serving as orderly for General Samuel Patterson of the Delaware militia. An epidemic, called at the time "malignant fever," swept through the city and Deborah was stricken. At a hospital, lying unconscious, she could do nothing further to maintain her disguise. The staff surgeon, Dr. Binney, while making his rounds, noted her labored breathing. Reaching inside the soldier's tunic he was startled: even the tight bandages could not hide the swell of a woman's breast. For reasons not noted, Dr. Binney kept the secret until Deborah recovered. Then the good doctor's niece became smitten with the soldier, and only an expedition west of the mountains with General Patterson and a skirmish with Indians saved Deborah from further exposure. But when Private Shurtleff arrived back east, the niece renewed her protestations of affection, so Dr. Binney decided he had had enough of the charade. He told the story to General Patterson who in turn told General Washington. Deborah was given an honorable discharge.

There was however, one final bit of drama. General Patterson, with the war's troubles largely over, indulged in a bit of playfulness. Telling the girl to dress in her rightful clothes, he walked with her on his arm past the mustered ranks of the 4th Massachusetts. Not one of her former companions recognized Deborah Sampson. The Hudson Valley did not see the woman warrior again until she had married, borne three children, and taken to the lecture platform. Congress and her home state of Massachusetts both gave her a bonus and Congress granted her a pension in recognition for her wartime service.

Or, to cite another forgotten name, who remembers Mrs. Hannah Lord Montague? She lived in Troy during the first decades of the nineteenth century, raising children and keeping house as millions of other women were doing. But Hannah tired of washing the collars of her husband's shirts when the rest of the garment was still unsoiled. Out of her annoyance came the idea for the detachable collar: by 1829, a new industry was born and Troy was on the way to becoming the shirt capital of the East. When detachable cuffs followed, the boom was on.

Not far away, in Rensselaer, one finds Fort Crailo whose chief claim to fame, according to local legend, lies in the fact that in 1758 an English army surgeon, Dr. Richard Shuckburgh, on his way with troops to attack Ticonderoga, sat on the well curb by the side door and composed "Yankee Doodle" to poke fun at the provincial soldiers training nearby. Twenty years later, it became the marching song that lightened the hearts of many American patriots.

If a stroller through the pages of history continues southward toward Millbrook, he will find the home of the Secretary of the Navy who wrote a single line of doggerel more famous than any of his official actions. His name was James Kirke Paulding, and he was a close friend of Washington Irving, with whom he collaborated in publishing the *Salmagundi* papers. Years later, Martin Van Buren, whose home was in Kinderhook, invited Irving to be his Secretary of the Navy and when the author of *Rip Van Winkle* and *The Legend of Sleepy Hollow* begged off, Paulding took the post. Navy men may remember how he defended sails against steam, but everyone—especially children—repeats the line he wrote, "Peter Piper picked a peck of pickled peppers," without having any idea of its origin.

There is an old home in Fishkill Landing called the Colonel John Brinckerhoff House that in recent years has become a Finnish rest home and center for Finnish athletes. Of all the guests who have stayed there, only a handful know the delightful legend of the original owner and his attempts to pry information out of General George Washington. The hero of the Revolution was a frequent guest at the Brinckerhoff place where, the story runs, his hostess tucked him in every night. This obviously did not displease the general, nor apparently her willing husband. But when the latter tried to elicit military information from his honored guest, Washington asked,

"Can you keep a secret?"

"Yes, indeed," said Brinckerhoff, eagerly.

"So can I, sir," replied Washington, ending their colloquy.

Near Athens the Livingstons planned a new city which they called Esperanza, giving the streets such optimistic names as Hope, Happiness, Equality, and Liberty. Nor did they forget more earthy names like Cider and Beer. Yet, after they sold a few building lots, the district was absorbed into the town of Athens—and that dream died aborning.

Between the communities of Coxsackie and Catskill there is a small house that testifies to the stout heart and firm mind of one of the early residents. It is the Stepmother's House, attached to the Bronck House, now the headquarters of the Greene County Historical Society. According to local tradition, Judge Leonard Bronck, a descendant of that early Jonas Bronck after whom the New York City borough of the Bronx is named, had several daughters by his first wife. When the latter died he married again, but the daughters refused to live under the same roof with their stepmother. With Solomon-like wisdom, and a typical Dutch dislike for feminine quarreling, the judge built her a one-room brick house in the rear of the main dwelling, complete with stone fireplace, Dutch oven, tight cellar, and a stairway leading to the attic that could be drawn down from the ceiling with a rope pulley.

The Bronck daughters were not the only rugged individualists in that neighborhood. A century later, in 1873, John Burroughs, the naturalist and writer, built a stone house in West Park, with a magnificent view of the Hudson. Eight years later, annoyed by the growth of the area and the intrusions on his privacy, he built a one-room building called Bark Study. Even this was not peaceful enough for the noted conservationist and nature lover, so he built a third retreat called Slabsides, a little

216

BRONCK HOMESTEAD

This 1884 print of the Bronck homestead shows the Stepmother's House attached to the Bronck House, as well as several other farm buildings. All of the buildings in the complex except the two at the far right are still in use as museum units, maintained by the Greene County Historical Society.

217

farther to the west in the hills. When asked why he sought such solitude he said, "The lion-hunters are too numerous."Theodore Roosevelt, while President, rode up the Hudson to see him one July day and walked all the way from his steam yacht to Slabsides. Burroughs excluded Roosevelt from the category of lion-hunters because the President, an ardent conservationist, did so much to create parks and preserve the natural heritage of the country.

At Schuylerville, where the Saratoga Monument marks the victory over Burgoyne, there are four niches, three holding statues of Schuyler, Gates, and Daniel Morgan. The fourth, where Benedict Arnold's statue should be, is empty. A stone mason, working on this monument, incorporated a palm leaf instead of a rosette in Schuyler's niche. Feeling that on this earth nothing could be or should be perfect, as he hoped it would be in Heaven, the mason saw to it that this small imperfection would always support his theory.

In a sense, Newburgh is a shrine to our spirit of independence. It was at the military barracks of the New Windsor Cantonment outside the town that Washington scotched talk of taking over the civil government by military officers with some of the firmest and noblest words ever written. To those officers and men who sought by a coup to institute a military government, he promised that by altering their minds they would make it possible for posterity to say, "Had this day been wanting, the world had never seen the last state of perfection to which human nature is capable of attaining."

The Newburgh house where he maintained headquarters during the last months of the war, and where he prepared his answers to small bands of malcontents, still stands as it was when he and Martha shared it with his staff. It must have been a trying time for Martha Washington. She was indefatigable in trying to make life pleasant for the generals and younger officers on her husband's staff, but had very little room at her disposal. Often the large central room—a chamber with seven doors but only one window—served as a dormitory at night. Officers had to arise early and store their blankets away so that the space could

WASHINGTON'S HEADQUARTERS AT NEWBURGH

The house in Newburgh where George Washington maintained his headquarters during the last years of the war, from a steel engraving published in 1859 in the volume *Illustrations to Irving's Life of Washington*.

Sleepy Hollow Restorations

Martha Washington

Sleepy Hollow Restorations

MARTHA WASHINGTON

Martha Washington served as hostess and virtual innkeeper to the officers of her husband's staff who occupied the cramped quarters at Newburgh. This illustration is also from the *Illustrations to Irving's Life of Washington.*

be used for breakfast. Then some of the tables followed the blankets into hiding and the room became the conference hall.

Kingston residents rightly boast that independence was nurtured in their town as well. Striving during the Revolutionary War to keep out of the hands of the advancing British, New York State's temporary government fled in 1777 from the lower valley to Kingston. Meeting in the courthouse and in the building now known as the Senate House that dates back to 1676, the patriot officials managed, despite obvious military pressures, to adopt the first State Constitution, inaugurate George Clinton as the first Governor, impanel the first court jury to function under the new constitution, and hold the first session of the state legislature.

Dreams and independence were the warp and woof of many a personal tapestry woven by those who dwelt along the Hudson. Jeremiah Dobbs was motivated by both when he set out to ferry people from one side of the river to the other. A hundred and fifty years later John Ericsson, a guest in the home of John F. Winslow near Poughkeepsie, drew the plans for the Union Navy's ironclad "saltbox on a raft," the *USS Monitor*. Each man had a dream and saw it come to realization.

In a lighter, more fanciful vein, Washington Irving's dreams began beside the river, too. He was a young man when he visited the Van Alen homestead near Kinderhook after the death of his early love, Matilda Hoffman. There he walked and talked with Helen Van Alen, whose character seems to have inspired the fictional figure of Katrina Van Tassel, the heroine of *The Legend of Sleepy Hollow*.

It took dreams—and hard work—to change the blue clay under the surface of the land into brick, creating an industry that lasted many generations and for a time made the Hudson Valley the largest producer of common brick in the world. Or to peel the bark off thousands of hemlocks to get the natural acids used in tanning hides. Bark peelers moved into the forests where the Palatine Germans had hunted for naval stores a century before, and made a new business for the river dwellers. Freighters loaded with green hides from the Patagonian plains discharged

ICHABOD CRANE AND KATRINA VAN TASSEL

The itinerant schoolteacher Ichabod Crane, a central character in Washington Irving's *The Legend of Sleepy Hollow*, admiring the charms of Katrina Van Tassel, in an 1861 painting by the American artist Daniel Huntington (1816–1906).

their cargo at many a river town for transshipment to the tanneries that often hid the peaks of the Catskills with the yellow acrid smoke from their chimneys. And so it was with copper products, Portland cement, carpets and rugs, textiles, and so many other products manufactured along the Hudson.

Chapter XI

These Stately Mansions

Strung along the Hudson like gems in a magnificent necklace are many of the most historic and beautiful homes in America. A few remain for the most part as their owners, Dutch pioneers or nineteenth-century tycoons built them. Some have been restored, some altered a little, and some reconstructed. All hold within their walls memories of the great human drama that saw the white man's civilization come to the river valley, menace the beauty of the wilderness for generations, and then once again in our own time strive belatedly but energetically to restore that beauty.

They range from small stone farmhouses to ornate palaces modeled after the great homes of Europe. Unlike the castles on the Rhine errected primarily to provide safety, the structures along the Hudson were built so their owners might glory in the view and, in many cases, impress friends and enemies alike with their opulence. Obviously, the fact that the river provided a ready means of transportation was an important factor; but the personal histories of many of the owners reveal that the selection of their home sites was dictated mainly by the magnificence of the vistas they would enjoy. In a few cases, because of subsequent building encroachments, it is difficult to imagine what the surroundings were like two centuries ago. When Kings College was built in lower Manhattan in the 1750s, an English visitor said, "It will be the most beautifully situated of any college, I

224

STONE COTTAGE WHICH WAS TO BECOME SUNNYSIDE

When Washington Irving purchased the home which was later to become Sunnyside, it was but a small stone cottage which had been a tenant farmer's house on Philipsburg Manor in the late seventeenth century. This watercolor of the cottage previous to improvement is attributed to George Harvey (c. 1800/1801–1878), c. 1835.

believe, in the world." More than a century later when its successor, Columbia University, built its third home at 116th Street, it too possessed a magnificent prospect of the river. Now that view is hidden by highrise apartment buildings.

Philipse Hall in Yonkers, where the Philipse clan built their first manor house and gristmill, is now hemmed in with business buildings. Other homes have been more fortunate and stand today upon the river shores much as they did when first erected. In Tarrytown, one finds Washington Irving's little house, Sunnyside, restored as it was at the time the author lived there. Surely, it is one of the most picturesque homes in the country, a strange mixture of early Dutch farmhouse, Amsterdam town house, and pure Irving. Its stepped or crow's-foot gables were added at Irving's request, and later he himself drew the plans for an addition, three stories high, which resembles a pagoda.

Irving used to sit on his porch looking across the Tappan Zee and marvel at the beauty of the scene. So attractive was his home that it became a mecca for artists who at one time or another painted it in oils, watercolors, or crayon, or turned to lithography and photography to catch its moods in different seasons. Many an old house, famous in its day, has been restored with little of the original furnishings available, but Sunnyside is literally crowded with Irving's own belongings, from his desk and shaving kit to the square rosewood piano and dining-room furnishings. Were the author to see it today, he would agree with the verdict of Henry James:

> . . . there is even yet so much charm that one doesn't attempt to say where the parts of it, all kept together in a rich conciliatory way, begin or end—though indeed, I hasten to add, the identity of the original modest house, the shrine within the gilded shell, has been religiously preserved.

The onward march of growth and change has left the residential gems in the Hudson River necklace in a sort of natural disarray. Buildings that are neighbors today may have been built a century or more apart, leaving an early farm cottage close to an

PHILIPSE MANOR HALL, YONKERS

This 18th century watercolor of Philipse Manor Hall in Yonkers shows the site as it would have appeared when the Philipses built their first manor house and gristmill there. The drawing is dated "June 18th 1784" and marked "D. R. fecit" but the artist is unidentified.

WASHINGTON IRVING AT SUNNYSIDE

This photograph of Washington Irving at Sunnyside was made from an 1856 stereoscopic slide by F. Langenheim. Irving was 73 when the picture was taken.

ornate mansion of the post-Civil War period. Yet in this section of the Hudson Valley known as Sleepy Hollow Country, contrast has added to, rather than detracted from, the charm of the district. As an example consider the fact that Sunnyside's next-door neighbor is Lyndhurst, once the home of Jay Gould, Wall Street manipulator and business rival of Cyrus W. Field, Cornelius Vanderbilt, and other financiers. Built in 1840, for Philip K. Paulding, and later altered and enlarged, the mansion is a striking example of what the combination of money and the gifted architect, A. J. Davis, could achieve. This Gothic-revival structure, now owned by the National Trust for Historic Preservation, has touches that remind the viewer of a battlemented fortress and a Florentine palace.

How different, though, were the lives lived within these neighboring homes. Irving's existence was marked by disciplined hard work at his literary chores and relaxation with his relatives and friends. At Lyndhurst, Gould planned some of the coups that led to his near-corner of the gold market which contributed to the financial panic of Black Friday, September 24, 1869. Here dwelt his daughter, Mrs. Helen Gould Shepard, noted for her entertaining and philanthropies, and, at her death, another daughter, the Duchess de Talleyrand.

North again from Lyndhurst, in North Tarrytown, is Philipsburg Manor, Upper Mills, perhaps the most striking extant example of an early Dutch home and milling and trading complex. Built by Frederick Philipse, the carpenter who worked for the Dutch West India Company until he became the richest man in New York, it was the northern outpost for his huge ninety-thousand-acre manor. The house, of fieldstone, has been reconstructed to its original appearance with the help of archeological and documentary research. When Frederick Philipse built it, it had four rooms, two above the others. His son, Adolph, added four more by the simple method of duplicating his father's plans. Beside the millpond and dam stands the reconstructed mill, which never fails to fascinate the thousands of visitors who come from far and wide to see the massive grinding wheels turn corn into cornmeal. Some 250 years ago, Hud-

LYNDHURST

Lyndhurst, a stone Gothic-revival mansion, was designed by the noted American architect, A. J. Davis (1803–1892), built in 1840 for William Paulding, former mayor of New York City, and his son, Philip K. Paulding. It was later enlarged and occupied by financier Jay Gould.

PHILIPSBURG MANOR, UPPER MILLS

This oil painting of Philipsburg Manor, Upper Mills in North Tarrytown, by an unknown nineteenth century artist, shows the gristmill and fieldstone house at the site.

son River sloops tied up at the wharf adjacent to the mill to load meal, barrel staves, and lumber for markets as distant as Europe and Madagascar.

At Croton-on-Hudson sits Van Cortlandt Manor, seat of one of the outstanding patriot families in New York State. Pierre Van Cortlandt, who lived there before the Revolutionary War, became the first lieutenant governor of the new state and his son, Philip, as colonel in command of a New York State regiment, participated in many of the major battles of the conflict. Stephanus Van Cortlandt began building the headquarters home for his eighty-six-thousand-acre manor in 1680. It continued to be lived in for a span of 260 years by seven generations of Van Cortlandts, the last direct descendant of the old Lord of the Manor being Anne Stevenson Van Cortlandt, who died in 1940. For the next thirteen years, the house deteriorated and it was threatened with demolition when John D. Rockefeller, Jr., bought it to save it. Today it is one of three properties purchased with funds supplied mainly by the late Mr. Rockefeller maintained in the public interest by Sleepy Hollow Restorations, a nonprofit educational corporation founded by the philanthropist. The others are Philipsburg Manor, Upper Mills, and Irving's home, Sunnyside. Together, they span three centuries, like pages of history made tangible, bearing witness to the life that once existed in Sleepy Hollow Country.

Unfortunately, not all of the beautiful homes along the river could be rescued from the onward rush of progress. Perhaps the oddest story of all the efforts to save landmarks is that of Boscobel, the classic Robert Adam–style mansion now standing at Garrison, across from West Point. Boscobel, originally at Crugers, south of Peekskill and in from the river, was built in 1792 by Staats Morris Dyckman, a Tory who came home from England and was forgiven his sins. Dyckman did not live to see it completed, but his widow lived on in the uncompleted structure until her death. His granddaughter married into the Cruger family, completed construction of the mansion and named it. In the 1840s and '50s, it was a social center for the region. Soon after World War I, however, the last Cruger moved away.

232

VAN CORTLANDT MANOR HOUSE

The Van Cortlandt Manor House, c. 1841, engraved by
Augustus Fay after F. A. Chapman (1818–1891), originally
published in *A History of Westchester County*, by Robert
Bolton, Jr. (New York, 1848).

Westchester County bought the land and turned it into Crugers Park but was kept from demolishing Boscobel by the cries of outraged neighbors. After World War II, doom seemed even more imminent when the Park Commission sold the place to the Federal Government for a mental-hospital site. Year after year thereafter the magnificent house sank further into disrepair. Mentally disturbed patients hid out in the cellar and the boys of the district learned that by flooding the main-floor rooms in winter they could have an indoor skating rink. The federal authorities in Washington declared Boscobel surplus property and sold it for $35 to a house wrecker.

Thereupon, Putnam County Historical Society members marched to the site and kept the wreckers from attacking the structure with iron ball and crowbar. State police were called in. At that juncture, Lila Acheson Wallace, wife of DeWitt Wallace and co-publisher of the *Reader's Digest*, provided $500,000, the Reader's Digest Foundation a similar amount, and the house was removed, piece by marked piece, to the present site on a knoll overlooking the Hudson.

Detailing the painstaking work of rebuilding the house would fill the pages of a good-sized book, but the effort was not in vain: it saved a landmark. During ceremonies dedicating the restored mansion, Nelson A. Rockefeller, then New York's governor, summed it up in these words: "The rebuilding of Boscobel restores to our Hudson Valley one of the most beautiful homes ever built in America." The name Boscobel was a simplification of the Italian *bosco bello* or "fair wood," an appropriate name indeed for such a house.

While most of the great houses date back to a much earlier era, few equal in fame or are more frequently visited by the public than the home of President Franklin D. Roosevelt at Hyde Park. Built as a small clapboard farmhouse in 1826, it was bought by the President's father in 1867 and enlarged and improved almost continually until the Summer of 1916. The present structure has fifty rooms and nine baths: its fieldstone wings almost overwhelm the older central core; and it commands a view of the river that is truly breathtaking. While still alive, President

234

BOSCOBEL

Boscobel, the classic style mansion built for Staats Morris
Dyckman, was moved from Crugers to a knoll overlooking the
Hudson at Garrison, New York, where it now stands.

Roosevelt gave his home and the surrounding acreage to the nation, and then followed with an additional bequest of all his papers and more land upon which to build a library. Today the library with its museum extension, built by the Federal Government, is one of the most important archives in the land, used by scholars and historians from around the world. But the home itself is a shrine beloved by millions. In a rose garden at one corner of the mansion, the former President and his wife are buried near a simple stone that gives their names and the dates of their births and deaths—nothing else.

In the same town of Hyde Park, another famous house epitomizes the differences between the democratic Franklin D. Roosevelt and the aristocratic Vanderbilt family. The Frederick W. Vanderbilt mansion designed by McKim, Mead and White, one of the most prestigious architectural firms in American history, when completed in 1898, was acclaimed as one of the finest homes in Italian Renaissance–style in the world. Decorated lavishly, it is a symbol of its times: nothing but the best went into the construction and furnishings.

The lawns and plantings reflect the zeal with which former owners of the property improved the site. Lord Cornbury, the old royal governor of the province, had owned it for a while; then Dr. John Bard, physician to George Washington, and his son, Dr. Samuel Bard, possessed it, setting out fine trees to please future generations. Subsequently, John Jacob Astor bought it for a daughter whose son sold it to Frederick W. Vanderbilt. When Vanderbilt erected his mansion he made full use of the earlier plantings and landscaping on this seven-hundred-acre estate, with its magnificent vistas across the Hudson to the Shawangunk and Catskill Mountains. Much of the landscaping is the work of the Belgian André Parmentier, one of the earliest professional landscape gardeners in the United States. As the home and estate are now public, under the supervision of the National Park Service, visitors may see how multimillionaires lived in that gilded age before World War I.

One of the oddest decorative touches in the house is the ceiling of one of the main rooms. It is a mural showing pretty,

FRANKLIN D. ROOSEVELT HOME AT HYDE PARK

"Springwood," the home of Franklin D. Roosevelt in Hyde Park, painted as it appeared before 1915 by I. V. Lounsbery.

VANDERBILT MANSION, HYDE PARK

Original architect's drawing of the Frederick W. Vanderbilt
Mansion, as rendered in 1895 by the prestigious American
architectural firm of McKim, Mead and White. The Roosevelt
and Vanderbilt homes in Hyde Park are now maintained as
National Historic Sites by the United States Department of the
Interior.

MARTIN VAN BUREN HOMESTEAD, "LINDENWALD"

This photograph of "Lindenwald," the Martin Van Buren homestead in Kinderhook, New York, dates from the early twentieth century. Subsequent owners of the house added a southern colonial portico extended across the front, replacing the Van Buren Victorian entrance shown here, and a screened porch.

View of Bryant Place by Hooker.

240

SCHUYLER MANSION, ALBANY

General Philip J. Schuyler called his Albany mansion "The Pastures" because his large estate overlooked pasture land sloping down to the Hudson. The house was originally completed in 1762 and occupied by the General until his death in 1804. Late in the eighteenth century, a hexagonal entrance porch was added to the house. The porch is visible in this watercolor rendering of the Schuyler Mansion c. 1818 by Philip Hooker (1766–1836). The house at this time was owned by a Mr. Byran, hence Hooker's inscription "View of Byrans Place" on the illustration on page 240.

bare-bosomed nymphs gamboling about the figure of a dejected old man who bears more than a little resemblance to Rodin's *The Thinker*. Decorators are said to have finished the ceiling before Vanderbilt and his wife saw it; when they did, they were so upset by the painting that they ordered it hidden under several layers of whitewash. When the Federal Government took over the property, workmen cleaned the rooms and in the process discovered the mural under the whitewash. Less puritanical than the former owners, the National Park Service ruled that the painting should remain visible for what they called "historical and interpretative reasons."

A much less expensive but equally famous house is Lindenwald, the home of President Martin Van Buren in Kinderhook. Built in 1797, it was a fine example of late Georgian architecture; but, during the Victorian period, the exterior was covered with gingerbread, outsized dormers, and other jigsaw decoration. Fortunately, the interior is still largely untouched and unspoiled. After Judge William Peter Van Ness, its builder, died, his son William took over. It was with Judge Van Ness that Martin Van Buren studied law. The younger Van Ness was a great friend of Aaron Burr and served as his second in the duel in Weehawken in 1804 when Alexander Hamilton was fatally shot. Hated and condemned by the public, Burr spent much time in this house in Kinderhook. Another frequent visitor was Washington Irving, who served as tutor to the Van Ness children in his younger days. After his term as President ended in 1840, Martin Van Buren bought the house and lived in it the rest of his life.

There are several fine homes north of Albany, including two Schuyler landmarks, each rich in history. Schuyler House in Schuylerville, the country home of General Philip Schuyler, was where his wife, Catherine, burned the wheat to keep it from falling into the hands of the British during the Revolutionary War. After which Gentleman Johnny Burgoyne burned it to the ground. Rebuilt after the war, it is a pleasant rural structure with a wide porch two stories high. But it is Schuyler's town house in Albany, known as The Pastures, that stands today as a major landmark. Schuyler was a prominent leader among those seeking independence through appeals to reason and justice, but when those failed, he fought just as hard for military victory. He served in the Continental Congress, was one of the first two United States senators from New York, and also served as chairman of the Board of Indian Commissioners.

The Pastures is one of the finest examples of American Georgian architecture to be found in the world. Its great gallery, where balls were held and notables entertained, is a striking example of early American workmanship. In this house Elizabeth Schuyler was married to Alexander Hamilton, the only one of the general's many daughters, it is said, who did not elope by climbing out of the window or in some equally romantic manner. Here, too, Burgoyne was entertained after his surrender and apologized profusely for having burned the summer home.

On one occasion, when local Tory ruffians who assumed the name of "Cowboys" sought to kidnap General Schuyler for ransom in Canada, they obtained help from Indians and half-breeds for the abduction attempt. On a hot, sultry August afternoon, the outlaws struck. The general and his family barricaded themselves in the upper rooms but at the last minute the women remembered that an infant granddaughter was asleep in a crib downstairs. Margarita Schuyler raced down, grabbed the baby, and fled back up the stairs just as an Indian flung his tomahawk at her. It missed and imbedded itself in the mahogany handrail. Meanwhile Schuyler shouted from a window as though to command a military company surrounding the house, and the attackers fled, carrying off some of the silver. New York State now owns The Pastures and visitors to the home can still see the deep gash left by the tomahawk.

A few more of the many famous or beautiful houses on both sides of the river deserve special mention for their historic roles. One is the Senate House in Kingston, where John Jay and others drafted the first State constitution. Here too the Senate met when there was no room in the courthouse—the temporary seat of State government. Originally an old Dutch house, it is a

243

SENATE HOUSE, KINGSTON

Originally an Old Dutch house, the structure now known as the Senate House in Kingston was the site where the first State constitution was drafted and where the Senate sometimes met during the period when Kingston served as the seat of State government.

New York State Department of Commerce

story-and-a-half high, much longer than it is wide, built in the typical Dutch farmhouse style of native blue limestone. As with so many of these old houses, age seems only to have improved its appearance.

The houses that make up the old Huguenot village in New Paltz had colorful beginnings. In 1663, Indians raided the earlier village of Hurley, making off with many captives, mostly women and children, including the wife and children of a Huguenot leader, Colonel Louis DuBois. A rescue party led by DuBois set out immediately and was unusually successful, overtaking the Indian band and retrieving the captives. Although distraught at the thought of what might be happening to his family, DuBois could not help noting the pleasant appearance of the verdant countryside through which the rescuers were hurrying. After the rescue was accomplished the colonel and several companions sought permission to buy the land from its Indian owners. The new English government agreed and the Huguenots purchased homesites at New Paltz. Before long they had built a street of stone houses, some of them with loopholes cut in the walls in the event other Indians returned with hostile intentions.

New Paltz has grown up around Huguenot Street without invading it; so it remains as it was built around 1710, a lived-in museum of uncommon value because of its freedom from later changes. The Jean Hasbrouck house still has the secret room designed to serve as a hiding-place if the Indians threatened, as well as a place for cockfights in the kitchen. For half a century the Huguenots enjoyed self-rule within the confines of an English province, while surrounded by people who were almost all Dutch. Their life was characterized by one observer as "fine and free from animosity and greed."

These houses and public structures, along with others of similar importance, are symbols. They are also tangible evidence of the styles of architecture and ways of life in early days, indispensable backdrops to an understanding of our historical heritage.

One can stand in Irving's Sunnyside home and imagine he is listening to the author practicing on his flute, or walk across

SUNNYSIDE, BY GEORGE INNESS

Washington Irving's Tarrytown home, Sunnyside, lies in the heart of the Sleepy Hollow Country which he made famous in his writings. This nineteenth century oil painting is by George Inness (1825–1894).

the milldam at Philipsburg Manor, hear the great waterwheel splashing, and see in his mind's eye the golden meal being sacked and transferred to sloops bobbing at the wharf below. The missing Delft tiles in the Van Corlandt Manor house at Croton, stolen by guerrillas to use as plates; the tomahawk cut in the handrail at the Schuyler home; the loopholes for muskets in the stone houses in New Paltz—all these are fragments of our history. Less important perhaps, but also shedding light on the kind of people who lived along the Hudson, is the Old Turtle House at Hudson, built by a sea captain so he could "walk the deck" without leaving the house.

Few regions can boast of a greater variety of architecture than exists along the Hudson's banks, where a visitor can "see" and touch and sense so intimately the history of more than three centuries of human enterprise.

Chapter XII

Back to the Sources

When Henry Hudson's long boat returned to the *Half Moon*, after its short run above Albany, bringing word that there was no hope of finding further navigable water, the upper reaches of the Hudson were, for many years, doomed to near oblivion. The 150-mile stretch from Albany to the sea, virtually "an arm of the Atlantic," blossomed historically; but the northern half of the river's length remained unnoticed for the most part.

The reasons for this disparity were many and diverse. A navigable river creates history; one that cannot be traveled upon is of lesser significance. Then, too, the area around the upper Hudson was, for a time, a no-man's-land, an arena of constant strife between the French in Canada and the English in New York. War parties traversed the region on the way to and from battles; but in between these forays the formidable Adirondacks remained secluded, even the Indians preferring to live in the pleasant valleys.

Here and there the white man's civilization did penetrate the wilderness above the junction of the Mohawk and Hudson rivers. Military outposts were built at Fort Edward, Fort George, and Fort Ticonderoga. General Schuyler purchased great tracts of land north of Albany and built his country home near the site of the Battle of Saratoga. Lumbermen moved north along the Hudson, where it is a winding turbulent stream with cataracts and narrow gorges, cutting down logs and sending

FORT EDWARD

This aquatint engraving of Fort Edward by John Hill
(1770–1850) after William Guy Wall was included in the *Hudson
River Portfolio*, published in New York by Henry Megarey in
several editions between 1820 and 1828.

them downstream in huge rafts. For a time Glens Falls was the center of the lumbering industry, but in the Revolution the British, finding it in the direct path of their invasion, burned it to the ground. Even history was having difficulty getting a toehold on the upper Hudson.

When the fighting died down and commerce between Canada and New York became profitable, the northern reaches of the Hudson benefited little, inasmuch as travelers left the river at Fort Edward to make their way overland to Lake Champlain and the River Richelieu route. No one even knew where the Hudson's source was until 1837, more than 225 years after Henry Hudson discovered the river.

That enthusiastic French soldier and traveler, the Marquis de Chastellux, gives us a fascinating early view of this region, based on his trip there in 1780. Out of exaggeration or perhaps true awe, he termed the cataract at Cohoes, a "thundering 70-foot torrent," one of the scenic wonders of the world. In those days, crossing the river in winter was no simple matter. The Marquis negotiated the crossing with only one sleigh in his party breaking through the ice. His description, however, is rather harrowing:

> It is a very common accident, and is dealt with in two ways. One is to drag the horses onto the ice, if possible with the help of a lever or plank to lift them up. The other is to strangle them with their halter or the reins: as soon as they have lost their breath and motion, they float on the water, and are then hauled by their forefeet onto the ice.

At Glens Falls he found the cataract more menacing than the one at Cohoes, saying that here the Hudson "frets and fumes, it foams and forms whirlpools, and flies like a serpent making its escape, still continuing its threats by horrible hissings." He would find it much less awesome today, confined as it is within ugly industrial buildings and rather tawdry surroundings.

James Fenimore Cooper set one of the most dramatic scenes

GLENS FALLS

The rushing waters of the Hudson at Glens Falls are clearly
visible in this John Hill engraving, from the *Hudson River
Portfolio* of Hill and W. G. Wall.

of *The Last of the Mohicans* in the caverns beneath these falls.

Guidebooks which extol Niagara Falls, exhort travelers to see the Adirondacks and the Finger Lakes, and enthusiastically describe Lake Champlain, say little about the Hudson between Albany and the high mountains. Yet this stretch of the river is truly beautiful, whether meandering through fertile valleys around Stillwater, Schuylerville, and Mechanicville or rushing downhill over rocky ledges around Hudson Falls, Glens Falls, and Warrensburg where the Schroon River adds its tumbling, frothy waters. Farther north, the Hudson becomes harder to follow. In the mountains, it becomes more turbulent, rushing through a gorge at Hadley's Falls, to quiet down at Thurman for a brief respite, and then grow wild at a rapids called the Horse Race. As the stream becomes smaller in the high hills, it passes through an area still known only to lumbermen, hikers, and other stout-hearted, strong-legged lovers of the outdoor life. It passes by places with such romantic names as Bad Luck Pond, Indian Lake, Vanderwhacker Mountain, and the Flowed Land. For a brief moment it cuts through a valley wide enough for a state highway to cross it, but from there on it winds through the wilderness where only a dirt road seeks to follow. At Henderson Lake even this road comes to an end.

Long before the white man came to North America, an Indian trace ran through this jumbled mass of high, rugged mountain peaks, extending south from Lake Placid to the lower ridges near Indian Lake. The white man, unless he were an engineer, must have wondered why the natives chose such a precipitous trail. Actually, this wilderness trace was the most direct route between the rivers flowing into the St. Lawrence and those leading into the Mohawk and Hudson. Any other trail would have added scores of miles to the trip. Not until the 1830s did anyone bother with this wilderness. Then a handful of men opened an iron mine at Henderson Lake, within a few miles of the headwaters of the Hudson, but they were too busy to be concerned with the birthplace of a great river.

In 1836, William L. Marcy, then New York's governor, decided that it was time for a geological survey of all the regions "back of beyond," so as to ascertain the State's resources. A distinguished Williams College professor of geology, Ebenezer Emmons, and his assistant, James Hall, were given the most rigorous assignment of all—to map, explore, and report on the territory in the heart of the Adirondack wilderness. There was a sort of divine justice in the selection of a Williams College professor for this exploration that definitely established the source of the Hudson.

Long before, on the morning of September 8, 1755, the British had fought a French force near Lake George. One of the British leaders had been Colonel Ephraim Williams, who had a presentiment of disaster on his way to the scene. At Albany the colonel drew up a will bequeathing most of his property to found a free school at Williamstown, Massachusetts. Williams was killed in that battle; thirty years later his bequest formed the first endowment for the creation of Williams College.

Emmons and Hall started their exploration at Port Henry on Lake Champlain, moving westward through the region north of Schroon Lake. Eventually they reached the iron mines at McIntyre, a crude settlement recently established between Lakes Henderson and Sanford. The proprietors of the ironworks offered them hospitality and their services as guides, but it soon became evident that they knew little more than the geologists about the actual headwaters of the Hudson.

Throughout this first expedition they labored under the misapprehension that the Opalescent River was the main branch of the Hudson. Hence they followed it through a gorge between Calamity and Cliff Mountains, breaking through virgin wilderness. Their dog was badly mauled by a panther. Deer and moose tracks were everywhere and on one occasion they broke into a clearing so unexpectedly that they flushed two wolves feasting on the carcass of a deer. Finally, they reached another lake, which they named after a friend, David C. Colden. It would appear from their reports that they believed this lake to be the actual source of the Hudson.

For some reason never made clear, they carried no instruments to establish the height of points above sea level; so when this expedition was called off for bad weather, they estimated that Lake Sanford was eight hundred feet above sea level and Lake Colden half again higher. The next summer's expedition corrected this error. That next summer, a larger party entered the wilderness from the iron forge, splitting up into sections to follow different streams. It was August when they began the final assault on the high peaks after ice formed on the water in their cooking-pans because of the low temperatures at high altitude. They ascended partway up the highest peak in the region, which they later named Mount Marcy for the incumbent governor. This time their instruments showed them that Marcy was 5,344 feet above sea level, far higher than anything in the Catskills, which until then were supposed to be the highest ranges in the state. Now they understood why the Indians called it *Tahawus* (He splits the sky).

Days of wandering and collecting geological samples took them into mid-August. When the expedition left the mountains the members were not agreed upon the actual source of the Hudson, some believing it was Avalanche Lake above Lake Henderson and some holding out for small streams feeding the Opalescent. Had the party turned off and ascended a small stream called Feldspar Brook, they would have found an even smaller lake higher on the flank of Mount Marcy. This small body of water was not to be discovered until much later, but the Emmons party did find that the headwaters of small brooks flowed two ways from a single area of about two square miles— some feeding the Hudson and others the Au Sable, which eventually carries water from Mount Marcy's other slope to Lake Champlain, the Richelieu, the St. Lawrence, and so to the Atlantic far north of the Hudson's mouth.

In 1872 Verplanck Colvin, a lawyer and topographical engineer, did follow Feldspar Brook to its source, where he found a tiny lake resting like a jewel in a mountain glen. There could no longer be any question about it: at 4,293 feet above sea level, this was the highest source of the water that plunges down the Adirondack flank, through the placid countryside around Albany, under the frowning steeps of the Highlands and the

SOURCE OF THE HUDSON

High in the Adirondacks, small brooks flow from Lake Tear of the Clouds to feed the Hudson. This illustration, entitled "Source of the Hudson," by Harry Fenn (1845–1911), evokes the sort of scene which might have been encountered by the earliest explorers of the region.

Palisades, to make its way finally into the Atlantic off New York City. Appropriately, one of the peaks in the Adirondack chain now bears Colvin's name. Emmons and Hall and, later, Colvin were all amazed at the views from the crest of Mount Marcy and other cloud-piercing mountains in the central Adirondacks. Gazing northward they could see clear to the broad alluvial plain through which the St. Lawrence cuts. To the northeast the shining surface of Lake Champlain was easy to identify, with the sturdy Green Mountains of Vermont framing it to the east. On clear days they could look toward the south and see the foothills of the Adirondacks where they disappeared near the fertile lowlands sweeping down to the Mohawk.

William C. Redfield, who accompanied the second Emmons and Hall expedition, was the first writer to inform the general public about the lonely majesty of the central Adirondacks, where a virgin wilderness existed at a point so little removed in actual mileage from the steamboat docks, the noisy towpaths of the Erie Canal, and the deafening industrial sounds of the furnaces in the gun factory at Watervliet, the looms of Troy, and the shipyards at Albany. Venturesome men, intrigued by Redfield's descriptions of mountain scenery—especially by the fact that on a clear day his party had been able to see the White Mountains of New Hampshire through a hogback in the Green Mountains—made their way into the Adirondacks on scouting expeditions. These expeditions have continued down to the present. But in the absence of funicular railways and cable cars, the ascent of Mount Marcy is still arduous enough to turn back most visitors except experienced hikers.

Consequently, for most of the year, silence reigns over and around the source of the Hudson, as if nature herself were eager to protect that tiny body of clear water known as Lake Tear of the Clouds.

Epilogue

In the span of three and a half centuries, the Hudson, which early explorers cited for its crystal water, was changed into a massive open sewer, polluted by raw sewage, industrial wastes, spilled oil, acids, and other chemical refuse. Despite the beautiful words written about its pristine majesty and the magnificent paintings depicting its charm, industry, vacationers, tourists, and the local residents themselves transformed it for a time into a noxious ditch. Into it was tossed everything unwanted: from a shipload of spoiled pork to industrial wastes, from human excreta to abandoned automobiles. Many people behaved as if there were no bottom to the river.

For decades it seemed that there was no end to the pollution of the Hudson; that before human beings, particularly those in industry, were done with it, it would be an ecologically dead stream, incapable of giving or supporting life. All of this happened, with very few exceptions, in the enlightened twentieth century. Damage wrought in the first half of the century was worse than anything that had been done since the creation of the Hudson in the Ice Age. Indeed, tragedy came to the river almost without public awareness.

Earlier times must have been idyllically pleasant for lack of any pollution as we know it. Homes, boats, wagons, fences, and furnishings were fashioned of wood which decayed when no longer serviceable. Vegetables, fruits, meats all came to market "naturally," without the need of plastic packaging. To the Indians and the white settlers a wood-chip basket sufficed for carrying most things, and it too decayed when broken and discarded. Even the metal tools, hinges, blades, weapons, wagon-wheel rims, and other implements, if abandoned, would rust away with the passage of the years. Household waste enriched the soil, and the environment suffered little from the effects of daily life.

The first baneful intruder was glass, which will not easily disintegrate. Then came metal alloys, defying rust and decay. Capping them all came plastics, most of them totally non-biodegradable, destined to join the aluminum beer can as the successor to the wild anemone, the mountain laurel, and the stately cattail along the river's edge. As if all this were not harmful enough, building contractors raped the magnificent escarpments rising from the Hudson's shore, especially on the western bank. Mountains were whittled down for traprock and paving blocks, stone to make cement, and sand for a thousand uses. Hills were ravished for soil to make brick, forests destroyed for their lumber or the tanning chemicals in their bark, without replanting or reforestation programs. Up and down the length of the valley there was a constant sound of blasting, as though the guns of war were firing in a never-ending battle.

In the long run, such destruction may have served to save the river, for the damage could be clearly seen. It was not like the pernicious poisoning of the water by unseen chemicals. People saw beauty being destroyed and, in due course, they took resolute steps to halt the gutting of one of the world's most beautiful scenic areas. Wealthy individuals as well as small groups of concerned citizens without great financial resources rallied against the despoilers. Money was sought from those who could afford to back their interest with tangible help.

It came from J. P. Morgan, the Harrimans, and the Rockefellers. It came, in amounts that were smaller individually but substantial in the aggregate, from thousands of others; so by the 1920s the last quarries had ceased their incessant blasting and dynamiting. After the Palisades, extending from opposite Manhattan northward to Bear Mountain, were saved, John D. Rockefeller, Jr., acquired the land on top of the escarpment to protect the skyline, and then gave the acreage to the bi-state Palisades Interstate Park Commission.

This was a great battle won. But the war still goes on, unflaggingly, along other reaches of the river. Perhaps the most important aspect of the fight against quarrying had been the realization, when it was over, that the public interest could serve in many ways to halt the despoiling of natural resources. Conservationists and environmentalists *could* stand up to corporate enterprises or government entities that appeared to act with no hint of conscience.

During World War II, for example, batteries were manufactured for the war effort at Foundry Cove near Constitution Island; in the process cadmium was dumped into the marshes north of the island as if it were no more dangerous than sugar. Scientists have asserted that in terms of disturbing ecological stability, mercury, itself a major pollutant, is nevertheless less harmful than cadmium.

One must never forget that the Hudson is the basis of much of the life that flourishes later in the Atlantic. Experts have called it the best estuarine area in the eastern United States. Without the young lives of thousands of species of life that begin in the Hudson the ecology of the whole area would be everlastingly altered.

Victories over the despoilers have come with increasing frequency as public awareness of the problem sharpened. One company was fined $200,000 for dumping harmful waste metals and acids in the Hudson. A second was subsequently fined for the same offense in Peekskill. Still another, without waiting for legal action, itself installed pollution-abatement equipment, and thus became the first large company voluntarily to clean up its operation.

No one should assume that the Hudson has been definitively saved. Nevertheless, within the last two decades it has staged a dramatic comeback. Sewage treatment increases with each passing month, and fishermen and scientists alike have noted the return, in impressive numbers, of many endangered species of marine life. There is now a large and articulate body of public opinion in the Hudson Valley, quick to protest, willing to turn to the courts for help and aware of their past victories. Enlightened corporate leaders have begun to see cooperation as the better part of valor.

The years ahead are full of travail for the Hudson. There is still considerable resistance to pollution control. However, it seems the battle to safeguard the Hudson *is* being slowly won, even if final victory is not yet assured.

The men, women, and even children, who have seen the recent improvement will not easily give up the fight. They know the joy of catching a striped bass or shad, the contentment of a canoe ride over water free from human debris, or simply the serenity that comes from seeing the river snake its way through magnificent mountain ranges, past lowland pastures, or under the frowning brow of the Palisades. They have made theirs the words of Henry James:

> Thus it was, possibly, that I saw the River shine, from that moment on, as a great romantic stream, such as could throw not a little of its glamour . . . over the city at its mouth.

The Hudson is a heritage beyond any mortal power to weigh, assay, or measure. Americans will not long stand by if ever again it is so dangerously threatened.

SLOOP *Clearwater*

With sails unfurled, the 106-foot-long sloop *Clearwater* is shown plying the Hudson River on a summer day. Used in environmental education and anti-pollution programs, the *Clearwater* has become a familiar symbol of continuing efforts to clean up the Hudson River.

Further Readings

Adams, Arthur G. *The Hudson River Guidebook*. New York: Fordham University Press, 1996.

Adams, Arthur G. *The Hudson Through the Years*. New York: Fordham University Press, 1996.

Amory, Cleveland. *The Last Resorts*. New York: Harper & Bros., 1948.

Bacon, Edgar Mayhew. *The Hudson River: From Ocean to Source*. New York: G. P. Putnam's Sons, 1902.

Barrett, Richmond. *Good Old Summer Days*. Boston: Houghton, Mifflin, 1952.

Beebe, Lucius. *The 20th Century: The Greatest Train in the World*. Berkeley, Calif.: Howell–North, 1962.

Boyle, Robert H. *The Hudson River: A Natural and Unnatural History*. New York: W. W. Norton, 1969.

Buckman, David Lear. *Old Steamboat Days on the Hudson River*. New York: Grafton Press, 1909.

Carmer, Carl. *The Hudson*. New York: Fordham University Press, 1992.

———. *My Kind of Country*. New York: David McKay Co., 1966.

Chastellux, François-Jean, Marquis de. *Travels in North America*. Chapel Hill: University of North Carolina Press, 1963.

Cook, Fred J. *What Manner of Men*. New York: Hastings House, 1963.

Eberlein, Harold Donaldson. *The Manors and Historic Homes of the Hudson Valley*. Philadelphia: J. B. Lippincott Co., 1924.

———, and Cortlandt Van Dyke Hubbard. *Historic Homes of the Hudson Valley*. New York: Architectural Book Publishing Co., 1942.

Folsom, Merrill. *Great American Mansions*. New York: Hastings House, 1963.

Fontenoy, Paul E. *The Sloops of the Hudson River*. Mystic, Conn.: The Mystic Seaport Museum in Association with the Hudson River Maritime Museum, 1994.

Harlow, Alvin F. *The Road of the Century*. New York: Creative Edge Press, 1947.

Hensen, Harry. *North of Manhattan*. New York: Hastings House, 1950.

The Hudson River, 1850–1918. Tarrytown: Sleepy Hollow Press, 1981.

Hungerford, Edward. *Men and Iron*. New York: Thomas Y. Crowell Co., 1938.

Further Readings

James, Bartlett B., and J. Franklin Jameson, eds. *Journal of Jasper Danckaerts, 1679–1680*. New York: Scribners, 1913.

Keller, Allan. *Colonial America*. New York: Hawthorne, 1971.

Kelley, Robert F. *American Rowing*. New York: G. P. Putnam's Sons, 1932.

Ketchum, Robert Glenn. *The Hudson River & the Highlands*. New York: Aperture, 1985.

Lossing, Benson J. *The Hudson: From the Wilderness to the Sea*. Troy, N.Y.: H. B. Nims & Co., 1866.

Mackesy, Piers. *The War for America*. Cambridge: Harvard University Press, 1965.

Martin, Joseph Plumb. *Private Yankee Doodle*. Boston: Little, Brown, 1962.

Milbert, J. *Picturesque Itinerary of the Hudson River*. Ridgewood, N.J.: Gregg Press, 1968.

Rajs, Jake. *The Hudson River*. New York: Monticelli Press, 1995.

Reigart, J. Franklin. *Life of Robert Fulton*. Philadelphia: C. G. Henderson & Co., 1856.

Riedesel, Frederika, Baroness von. *Memoirs*. Trans. William L. Stone. Albany: John Munsell, 1867.

Shaw, Ronald E. *Erie Water West*. Lexington: University of Kentucky Press, 1966.

Shultz, Gladys Denny. *Jenny Lind, the Swedish Nightingale*. Philadelphia: J. B. Lippincott Co., 1962.

Stanne, Stephen P. *The Hudson*. New Brunswick: Rutgers University Press, 1996.

Stevens, Frank Walker. *The Beginnings of the New York Central Railroad*. New York: G. P. Putnam's Sons, 1926.

Van Zandt, Roland. *The Catskill Mountain House*. New Brunswick, N.J.: Rutgers University Press, 1971.

———. *Chronicles of the Hudson*. Hensonville: Black Dome Press, 1992

Verplanck, William E., and Moses W. Collyer. *The Sloops of the Hudson*. New York: G. P. Putnam's Sons, 1908.

Waller, George. *Saratoga: Saga of an Impious Era*. New York: Bonanza Books, 1966.

Wilstach, Paul. *Hudson River Landings*. Indianapolis: Bobbs–Merrill, 1933.

WPA Guide to New York State. New York: Oxford University Press, 1940.

Index

267

Index

Index

269

Index

Index

271

Index